# 10 Lessons
# in Power
# Psychology

*Ten Practical Uses Of
Psychology That Just Might
Change Your Life!*

## Michael Abruzzese, Ph.D.

VISTA

*Vista Health Services, Inc.*

# 10 Lessons in Power Psychology

*Ten Practical Uses Of Psychology That Just Might Change Your Life!*

*by Michael Abruzzese, Ph.D.*

ISBN-13: 978-0-9910117-0-4
ISBN-10: 0991011708

Library of Congress Control Number: 2013954252

Vista Health Services, Inc.
PO Box 1060
Osterville, MA  02655 USA

*info@vistahealth.cc*

VISTA

## Here's What Others Are Saying About Dr. Abruzzese:

"Excellent material," *Rochester, NY*

"Well organized and presented," *Chicago, IL*

"Wish we could have had more time," *Newark, NJ*

"I learned a great deal from his workshop," *Amsterdam, The Netherlands*

"This workshop was great!" *San Francisco, CA*

"Stimulating and applicable to my clinical work," *Portland, ME*

"I was extremely satisfied by his presentation," *Mannheim, Germany*

"Dr. A. clearly knows this topic inside and out," *Salt Lake City, UT*

"Superb, as always," *Brookline, MA*

"More!" *Denver, CO*

"This instructor has rich information," *Corfu, Greece*

"He was excellent!" *San Jose, CA*

"Dr. Abruzzese is a very creative clinician. I look forward to 'the book'!" *New York, NY*

# *Our Better-Than-Money-Back Guarantee*

This book was written so readers could quickly and inexpensively learn Power Psychology techniques. If you decide it doesn't meet your needs, please send this book and your purchase receipt to us and we will refund **110%** of your purchase price. Suggestions for improving future editions are also welcome. Our address is:

Vista Health Services, Inc.
PO Box 1060
Osterville, MA 02655

VISTA

# Table of Contents

*"The happiness of your life depends upon the quality of your thoughts."*
—*Marcus Aurelius*

# Preface

This is a book about real estate. Seriously; it's about real estate. *Psychological* real estate.

That's because "psychology" is really nothing more than "land," like the land we walk on every day. It's like the land our parents built their homes on. Like the land the developers built the hospital on where we were born, or the roadway where the taxi stopped because it didn't make it to the hospital in time.

Or the land our apartment house was on where we got our first apartment. Or the land the school and college and office building were built upon where we went to school and got our first job. Or the land we'll build the skyscraper on when we make our first billion.

Land or buildings — it's all real estate. But nobody ever pays much attention to the land UNTIL the land starts to shift or move under them!

Psychology is just like that. It's the "land" upon which we "build" our lives, families and careers. And we don't pay much attention to it until it starts to shift and move under us!

Just like real estate — but VERY VALUABLE real estate indeed! And WE control it all, free and clear, with no bank mortgage to worry about! How great is that?

Psychology is monumental in its depth and breadth and it really IS the foundation upon which we build our lives. I was professionally educated at a time when it was expected that "Psychology" would be "given away" to as many people as possible, but the predominant model was the medical model of sitting in your office and treating patients one at a time.

Although I also taught at colleges and spoke to parent groups, it didn't take a genius to realize that no matter HOW many hours a week I worked, I could NEVER reach very many people because the knowledge I had was essentially "rationed" by insurance companies and income: Individuals needed the "right" kind of insurance or the ability to pay privately for office therapy or college classes.

So I decided to expand my practice to include websites, a free newsletter and books. This book is the first in a series of ten bringing Power Psychology techniques to people who might otherwise never know about them.

I chose to limit the contents of this book to just TEN LESSONS, sampling a wide range of areas that might be the most interesting and HELPFUL to a wide range of readers.

I also chose to write the lessons as BRIEF, REPETITIVE, ACTION PLANS that readers would ACTUALLY USE IMMEDIATELY, not just put away on a shelf for later.

I chose a writing format and style that was DIRECT, PLAYFUL and UNDERSTANDABLE to a wide range of readers, including older children.

YES: I know there are a LOT of annoying CAPITAL LETTERS — there are a lot of hyphens and short paragraphs, too — as well as other grammatical flairs (especially semi-colons) that I know some will find annoying, especially my colleagues who value GRAVITAS. It was kind of annoying to write this way, too, I'll admit, but I deliberately chose this format for the copy to influence as many different readers as possible.

So I decided to leave the GRAVITAS to others and keep the HELPFULNESS for my readers.

Let me know what you think.

*Michael Abruzzese, Ph.D.*
*DrA@vistahealth.cc*

*"There is nothing good or bad, but thinking makes it so."*

*–Hamlet*

# About the Author

Michael Abruzzese, M.A., M.A., Ph.D., H.S.P.P., is a licensed school psychologist, licensed clinical psychologist and health service provider specially trained to provide behavioral health care service to both children and adults. Dr. A. is also an author, radio host, college speaker and professional trainer.

He is a former Clinical Instructor at Harvard Medical School and part-time lecturer and Clinical Assistant Professor at Northeastern University. Dr. Abruzzese has also presented training workshops to other licensed health care professionals both nationally and internationally.

Dr. A. obtained advanced training in pediatric and adult neuropsychology and obtained specialized and post-graduate training in child psychology, community and cross-cultural psychology and crisis intervention and emergency psychological services.

He is also a Clinical Instructor at the Tufts University School of Medicine and he is listed in the National Register of Health Service Providers in Psychology. Dr. A. has testified over 200 times as an expert witness. For more information, please see *www.DrAPlus.com*.

*"The way of success is the way of continuous pursuit of knowledge."*
*–Napoleon Hill*

# Disclaimer

No book is the total authority on any subject and no person knows everything about everything — it is an impossibility in this age of instant and sometimes contradictory, if not downright and deliberately false, misinformation that is instantly available to people.

This book is designed to present a collection of chapters and information about self-help ideas and self-improvement suggestions and, as such, it cannot and does not constitute clinical or medical advice, nor diagnosis or treatment advice or recommendations.

No attempt has been made or is intended to provide a thorough or total review of the field of psychology, neurology, health or any other medical or educational field and the contents of these pages contain the opinions and suggestions by the author in a limited number of areas.

The book is not meant to replace or substitute individualized or other information publicly or privately available from other behavioral health sources, resources or individuals.

It is meant to provide educational and informational material that may encourage thought, entertain or suggest further areas for inquiry, research and help to the reader as may be appropriate, including the appropriate face-to-face clinical consultations with an appropriately educated, credentialed and licensed health care professional.

*"Books are the quietest and most constant of friends; they are the most accessible and wisest of counselors, and the most patient of teachers."*
*–Charles William Eliot*

# Acknowledgements

In accepting one of his several acting awards, Peter Falk remarked that it takes lots and lots of people working behind the scenes to permit a single person, fairly or not, to stand up and accept the award. Well, it takes a lot of people to produce a book, too — a LOT of people. But usually it's just the author who gets to put his or her name on the cover. It's hard for an author to look at a completed book without the urge to write acknowledgements that go on forever, because there are usually so many people whose comments, inspiration and support are part of any author's production.

While it's just not possible or feasible to cite in the allowable space permitted in this text all the research, authoritative works, conversations and other data that were reviewed and considered in preparation of this work, suffice it to say that it was voluminous and involved scores of colleagues, researchers, friends and professionals over the several drafts of this edition. To those whose names do not appear here, I hope you will realize it is due to forgetfulness or space limitations and not bad manners.

But I do want to especially thank my teachers, professors, patients and colleagues. I was fortunate to have teachers who encouraged me, from Miss Burke in Kindergarten, who kindly pointed me in the right direction so I could return home from the first day of school, to Miss Charter in the fourth grade, who taught me an awesome way to check for the correct answer to multiplication problems, to Mrs. Norton in the sixth grade, who encouraged my first articles for the school newspaper, to Mr. Jenny, my senior English teacher, who politely told me when my work stunk.

Regrettably, I haven't always been as diplomatic when critiquing some of my own students' work. Sorry, Mr. J.

I also want to thank my college, university and graduate professors, most of whom were interesting, well-intended and helpful, for instilling in me the belief that the practice of psychology is most importantly about discovering and imparting knowledge to others, not simply satisfying the constraints of insurance companies or the machinations of agency and organizational administrators or manipulators.

And I want to specifically thank the children, adolescents and families who have worked with me over the years for showing me what psychology can accomplish and for teaching me the difference between what psychology looks like in the laboratory and how it works in the real world. Each of them has had a role in the creation of this book.

I also want to thank Dee Netzel, my wonderful editor.

To my family, of course, go my loving and grateful thanks for patiently sharing the limited hours available during the days (and weekends) over the past months with TEN LESSONS.

And thanks to my Mom and Dad for their unceasing love and encouragement in all my endeavors and also for passing on their own love of words and writing, the value they placed on education and learning and the importance of helping others. I love you.

*"Knowledge isn't power until it is applied."*
—*Dale Carnegie*

# Chapter 1

## *How to P.A.C.E. Yourself!*

### *What Is "Power Psychology"?*

It is a simple solution to complex personal problems. Psychology is the science of understanding human behavior. Human behavior, of course, is complex and what seems obvious is not always the case. People have been studying — and trying to improve — human behavior since the philosopher Epictetus lectured in the public square of ancient Greece and it is often considered that the European struggle between religion and philosophy was the beginning of modern psychology.

In fact, some psychologists consider the Bible to be an excellent example of the practical uses of Power Psychology in that some sections contain clear and specific guidelines or rules about what to do and what not to do to achieve happiness, accomplish personal goals and avoid unpleasantness; that's very similar to some types of modern psychotherapy techniques!

But it wasn't until the emergence of modern philosophers in Europe and America that psychology became a separate discipline of learning and knowledge. Philosophers, such as William James, who taught at Harvard University in the 19th century, are often considered the direct "grandfathers" of modern psychology and nearly everybody knows the name of Sigmund Freud, the famous 19th century Viennese physician, who was among the first authorities to write and argue persuasively about "psychology" and how hidden and unsuspected psychological processes were actually responsible for all human behavior, including psychological "illnesses" such as "hysteria" and other conditions.

We've come a long way since then and modern science, such as Magnetic Resonance Imaging (MRI), Positron Emission Tomography (PET) and a veritable alphabet soup of other mechanical diagnostic assessment tools, has continued to show human behavior is, indeed, caused by "hidden psychological processes."

This is just a fancy way of saying that human behavior is the result of LOTS of previously unsuspected activities going on in the INSIDE of us WAY before any behavior shows up on the OUTSIDE of us!

And it's all these inside "things," made up of previously unsuspected physiological, cognitive and emotional activities that are responsible for much of the unhelpful, self-sabotaging and maladaptive behavior that is so destructive to our own happiness and psychological survival.

The GOOD news is that research by psychologists, neuroscientists and others shows that individuals can CHANGE many of the maladaptive behaviors that lead to psychological AND physiological problems that trouble so many people.

How to CHANGE THOSE BEHAVIORS is what this book is all about. Even better, each chapter is short, focused and self-contained, so you can read each chapter separately and still understand what is going on WITHOUT having to read all the other chapters first! How great is that?

OK, so that DOES means that I repeat A LOT of things over and over in each chapter that I also wrote here — but the REAL reason for repeating so much is that REPETITION is part of learning how to change behavior. So repetition is good — if it's the RIGHT TYPE of repetition, that is!

Power Psychology is simply a way of taking what scientists have found out in their laboratories about our "hidden psychological processes" and bringing it OUT of the laboratories and giving it to people in a way they can use in the real world. Why? So people can put "research" to use in their own lives to make real and

3

powerful changes in their own — and others' — behavior to improve the quality of their own lives — and the lives of the people they love.

Psychologists have taken the powerful psychological techniques from the research to the therapy office. I've drawn on these techniques and turned them into **Power Psychology Techniques for Living (PTL)**.

Power Psychology is simply a way for people to make REAL and POWERFUL changes in their OWN behavior and in the behavior of OTHERS with the goal of improving the quality of their own lives and the lives of the people whom they love.

## *And How Can Power Psychology Help?*

It can help YOU change your life for the better. Using **PTL** can help people overcome their personal obstacles, ease their tendencies towards self-sabotage and improve their ability to set and achieve goals.

The techniques are not complicated — Power Psychology is really very easy to use and almost impossible to screw up; however, you DO have to LEARN them, PRACTICE them and then USE them!

Or, to put it another way, you really have to DRIVE the car, not just buy it and leave it in the garage.

Once you KNOW the various techniques to use and practice, you just have to START USING them. The more you USE them, they get easier and easier to use!

4

## When Can I Get Started?

Right now. There are only four steps to learning any **PTL** — you just have to **P.A.C.E.** yourself.

**P** – You have to **PRACTICE**. This **PTL** was first revealed to me in graduate school by a toll booth collector on a highway in New York — who didn't happen to look like a philosopher, psychologist or scientific researcher, by the way — when I and several graduate school colleagues were on a road trip to the old Yankee Stadium. "How," I asked him, "do we get to Yankee Stadium?" He looked at me, slowly shook his head and then said, "Practice, practice, PRACTICE!"

---

*Psych Note! He was only half right. It's not just any old type of practice — you have to practice CORRECTLY. I learned this from a martial arts instructor — who also didn't look like a philosopher, psychologist or scientific researcher — when he looked at me, slowly shaking his head, and said, "Practice does NOT make perfect. PERFECT practice makes perfect." This got me to thinking: Why do people always slowly shake their heads when they speak to me? But I digress. The point is that one must not only LEARN a new technique, one must learn it and practice it CORRECTLY!*

---

**A** – You have to be **AWARE**. Like my trip to Yankee Stadium, you have to know something exists before you can do something about it. So, too, you must be **AWARE** of a behavior and its impact upon you before you can learn the right **PTL** to CHANGE the behavior.

And then you must be **AWARE** that YOU have the ability to CHANGE behavior by using the correct **PTL** — which is easy, because in ALL the **PTL** series, the necessary techniques are explained to you. You just have to know where to look . . . and this book is one handy place to look.

---

*Psych Note! Awareness is of VITAL importance. Most people are only dimly aware of what is really going on around them. That is because most people have TRAINED themselves to NOT pay attention to their own environment. PTL will show you why it is important to TURN OFF the "Do Not Pay Attention" switch and, instead, turn it ON!*

---

**C** – COGITATE. Well, this is really just a twenty-five cent word that really means "THINK!" (And what good is having a Ph.D. if you can't use a few fancy words now and then, right?) OK; I promise that's the last fancy word I'll use . . . for a little while, anyway; but you WILL see it again in this book! That's because we DO know from psychological research that THINKING is important!

Life-long learning, always learning new things and thinking about NEW ways to do old, familiar things, is the best way to ward off age-related memory loss and other poor thinking conditions. **PTL** is a teaching and learning experience and you DO have to think about what **PTL** can do for you. Not only will you learn new things, you may be able to train your brain to be smarter for a longer time!

Thinking is really important. There is no shame in thinking things through or being smart or using what you know, even if others around you don't.

*Psych Note!* Nobody can know everything and everybody knows things that other people don't, those are just facts of life. So it's OK to learn and grow as a person and it's also OK to show what you know to others and it's ALSO OK to learn what others have to show you, too. It's all part of being AWARE of what's going on around you.

E – EXPERIENCE it. **PTL** is about taking what science has learned in the laboratories and putting it to use in your own life, in the real world, starting today. You need to take what you learn from **PTL** and PUT IT INTO PRACTICE IN YOUR LIFE. Don't just cogitate, um, sorry; I mean: DON'T JUST THINK about what you've read so far, put it into practice — EXPERIENCE it.

Life is about experiences, not simply observations.

## So What Do You Want to Accomplish?

Where do you want **PTL** to take you? Your ability to improve areas of your life is usually limited by a lack of goals, dreams or desires. Make **PTL** an everyday part of your life for improvement in many little areas as well as big ones.

Start today — it all starts with you. It ALWAYS starts with you.

So let's get started and the next section is your first lesson. Right here. Right now, by doing a little assignment I have designed for you to do:

# *P. A. C. E.*

Simply start to **P.A.C.E.** yourself now — just by being **AWARE** of what's going on around you and in your life that you might like to improve upon.

**P**RACTICE being **AWARE** of what you want to improve upon and making lists is an excellent way to do that. **COGITATE** — think — about how you might like to change some things. And make a list — make many lists — because just the **EXPERIENCE** of making lists increases **AWARENESS** and helps you focus on what's important to you.

A WRITTEN list is much, much better than a list you just keep in your head. But only put THREE ITEMS on each of your lists — one list can be for work, another can be for home, family — whatever crosses your mind. Or just make one list — it's your choice. But make a list. As you THINK about things more, your list(s) may change. That's fine — just tear up the old list and make a newer, more accurate one!

That's essentially what the **EXPERIENCE** of thinking things through and making notes (in this example, those notes are put down as a list) is all about: THINKING; writing down what you have thought about in a list form; refining your thinking and your notes (your list); and doing it again. And again. And again. That's what repetition is all about: Practice, practice, **PRACTICE!**

## *T.A.F.N. . . .*

That's All For Now — whew, isn't that enough? Whenever you're ready for more, check out the next chapter in this **PTL** series that interests you or visit the website at www.TenLessons.org for more information. When you go to that site, you can click on some of the links there for more information about how psychology can help out in different aspects of life, overcoming obstacles and exceeding expectations.

---

*Psych Note! This introductory chapter sets forth the basics of all the PTLs to follow, but subsequent chapters in this book repeat much of the introductory information found here so that each subsequent PTL chapter can stand alone and they do NOT have to be read from first to last in order to be understood and effectively used. Use the sample list provided to start your first assignment. Seriously, writing things down is REALLY helpful in learning how to P.A.C.E. yourself.*

---

*The top 5 things I want to P.A.C.E. myself about are:*

1. Being a better parent

2. Increasing self awareness/ mindfulness

3. Eating + sleeping better

4.

5.

# *NOTES*

*"The health of nations is more important than the wealth of nations."*
*–Will Rogers*

# Chapter 2

## Using Power Psychology to Drop Up to 6 More Pounds This Month

### What Is "Power Psychology"?

It is a simple solution to complex personal problems. Psychology is the science of understanding human behavior. Human behavior, of course, is complex and what seems obvious is not always the case. People have been studying — and trying to improve — human behavior since the philosopher Epictetus lectured in the public square of ancient Greece and it is often considered that the European struggle between religion and philosophy was the beginning of modern psychology.

We've come a long way since then and modern science, such as Magnetic Resonance Imaging (MRI), Positron Emission Tomography (PET) and a veritable alphabet soup of other diagnostic assessment tools, has continued to show that human behavior is caused by "hidden psychological processes." This is just a fancy way of saying, "stuff we do that we usually don't think about very much."

Power Psychology is simply a way of taking what scientists have found out in their laboratories about our "hidden psychological processes" and bringing it OUT of the laboratories and giving it to people in a way they can use in the real world. Why? So people can put "research" to use in their own lives to make real and powerful changes in their own — and others' — behavior to improve the quality of their own lives — and the lives of the people they love. We take these powerful scientific psychological techniques and turn them into **Power Psychology Techniques for Living (PTL)**.

## How Can Power Psychology Help Me with My Weight Loss?

Using **Power Psychology Techniques** can help you change your life for the better. Applying **Power Psychology Techniques** to everyday actions and events in your life can improve results in so many areas — health, relationships, income, longevity — the list is probably only limited by your imagination.

This chapter, Chapter 2 in the series of **Power Psychology Techniques for Living**, focuses upon improving the results you can get from your weight loss program.

## When Can I Get Started?

Right now. There are always only FOUR STEPS to learning a particular set of **PTL**. Each chapter in the series is written to be a "stand-alone" chapter, which means that you can read each chapter alone and in any order you wish to learn the particular set of **PTL** that applies to the subject.

You don't have to read each chapter starting from the first in the series to the last in order to get a benefit from any chapter.

Each chapter builds on the previous chapters, however, and the more chapters you read, the more **PTL** you can learn to apply in your life. You can learn what you need to know about **PTL** for improving your WEIGHT LOSS — RIGHT HERE, RIGHT NOW.

This chapter doesn't give you a weight loss routine or diet because it assumes that you ALREADY HAVE a weight loss routine. This chapter helps you learn to use **PTL** to GET MORE out of the weight loss routine you already are using.

---

*Psych Note! If you don't have a weight loss routine or program now, I suggest you consider the Mediterranean Diet or the D.A.S.H. Diet. Both are rich in fruits, vegetables, nuts, beans, seeds, and heart-healthy fats and have reduced sodium content. But always consult your Primary Care Doctor or Primary Care Physician (PCP) about ANY "diet" before you start one.*

---

15

## *So Let's R.O.C.K. It . . . .*

Remember to **P.A.C.E.** yourself. That means, **P**RACTICE what you learn here; be **A**WARE of the environment in which you practice; **C**OGITATE (think) about what you are doing; and actually **E**XPERIENCE the four steps presented here, don't just read them and forget about them!

More about the basic **P.A.C.E.** process is discussed in my introductory Power Psychology chapter, Chapter 1 in this book. When you are ready, all you need to do next is **R.O.C.K.** the boat (YOUR boat, that is!).

**R** – REVIEW and **R**ECORD your diet. There are many diets available, of course, and mostly weight loss diets get all the publicity. But "diet" simply refers to what you eat on a daily basis.

The psychological aspects of weight loss, weight maintenance diets, and dieting is too lengthy a subject to review here, but I do write about **PTL** for diets in a separate Power Psychology article called "Using Power Psychology for Weight Management" (available at www.TenLessons.org). Always check with your doctor before making any changes in your diet, exercise and food intake routines.

You already have a diet, of course — it's whatever you put into your body on a regular basis! But is it healthy? Does it contain hidden sugar, saturated fats and salt? If so, then your diet is working against you.

The first step in LOSING weight — which is far different from KEEPING THE WEIGHT OFF once you lose it — is paying attention to what you are eating every day.

Don't change it — yet — just notice it. And by noticing it, I mean **RECORD** it: WRITE down what you eat — EVERYTHING you eat every day — for a week. That gives you your BASELINE. A baseline is from where you start and against which you measure your progress as you advance and make changes. So record what you eat.

---

*Psych Note! I know, I know . . . you're groaning about having to WRITE DOWN everything you eat. "Why? Why can't I just remember it all? Do I HAVE to really, actually write it all down?" Let me say this as gently as necessary: Yes. YES, YES, YES, YOU DO!! Why? I'll tell you at the end of the chapter — and it's a very good reason! Also remember to drink LOTS of water unless your doctor advises you otherwise.*

---

O – ORGANIZE your eating. That's right — put some organization into your eating! Don't skip ANY meals and don't work through your lunch hour. Take the time to plan WHEN you are going to eat and WHAT you are going to eat and then DO IT (and, when you've eaten it, of course, WRITE IT DOWN!).

Grabbing a bite any old time is a diet for disaster and you don't want that. You want to design a diet for success, don't you? Well, success takes work and effort — sometimes a lot, sometimes just a little: To lose up to an extra 6 pounds a month, it just takes a little effort on top of what you are already doing.

Don't forget — 6 pounds a month is only around a pound and a half each week and that's entirely doable. YOU CAN DO IT! Yes, YOU!

C – COGITATE. Well, this is a twenty-five cent word that I like to use, but it really just means "think" (so what good is having a Ph.D. if you can't use a few fancy words now and then?). We do know from psychological research that life-long learning and always learning new things are the best ways to ward off age-related memory loss and other poor thinking conditions.

What is more important, by THINKING about your diet and health repeatedly, you will likely find that you actually wind up DOING more to help improve your weight loss and health.

---

*Psych Note!* *Start using your imagination. That is, you have to VISUALIZE yourself recording your food intake and planning your meals and not skipping any meals. Going to work on the bus, train or subway? PICTURE yourself writing down what you eat that day and planning your meals. Waiting in line? PICTURE yourself planning meals, enjoying the meals you plan and recording what you eat, and LOSING THAT EXTRA POUND AND A HALF this week. All this IMAGINARY practice actually has a beneficial effect on your ACTUAL weight loss program.*

---

Don't underestimate the power of thinking — I know, THINKING seems SO unfashionable these days, but we know from YEARS of research that the more we THINK about things, the more we actually wind up DOING them — for better or worse . . . .

**K** – KEEP at it. **PTL** is about taking what science has learned in the laboratories and putting it to use in your own life, in the real world, starting today. You need to take what you learn from **PTL** and PUT IT INTO PRACTICE IN YOUR LIFE. Don't just cogitate, I mean — don't just think about what you've read so far — USE IT, DO IT, PRACTICE IT and do so CONSISTENTLY.

That means EVERY DAY. The more time you spend working on something and working on it CORRECTLY, the more likely you are to be successful. THINKING is very important and is ALWAYS a good place to start an activity, but thinking without ACTION will not change your life very much. It is the EXPERIENCE of putting our thoughts into action that improves our quality of life.

---

***Psych Note!*** *Actually, I'm being a little (and ONLY just a little) hard on you. Research indicates that, in reality, you don't really have to do new behavior every day to get a new benefit from it. Skipping a day is actually OK and will NOT destroy your progress. You just start from where you left off and DON'T obsess about having forgotten to write something down or visualize your weight loss.*

---

SO just keep moving forward; start doing it again and KEEP moving forward. What if you miss several days in a row or just plain STOP doing anything? Why then, just . . . START . . . over . . . again! **PTL** is a program where you can't lose — you can only win! If you forget once, just pick up where you left off and keep going forward. If you've stopped or dropped out — just start again. You can do this! Yes, YOU!

## *Your Turn Starts Now!*

**PTL** is about taking what science has learned in the laboratories and putting it to use in your own life, in the real world, starting today. You need to take what you learn from **PTL** and PUT IT INTO PRACTICE IN YOUR LIFE. Don't just THINK about what you've read so far — USE IT, DO IT, PRACTICE IT and do so CONSISTENTLY.

Remember, the more time you spend working on a task — working on it CORRECTLY, that is — the more likely you are to be successful at accomplishing that task. THINKING is very important and is ALWAYS a good place to start any activity, but thinking without ACTION will not change your life very much. It is the EXPERIENCE of putting positive thoughts into positive actions that can improve our quality of life. **PTL** is a program where you can't lose — you can just win. If you skip or miss a day or make a mistake, just pick up where you left off and keep going forward. If you've stopped or dropped out of a program — just start again. YOU CAN DO THIS! YES, YOU!

Little changes can produce large results. Prescription medicine and vitamins are measured in milligrams and sometimes micrograms, not POUNDS! Similarly, a little bit of behavior change can make a big difference in the quality of our lives.

All you need to get started is your brain — and, fortunately, you just happen to have it with you right now! How handy is that? Get that brain working and **RECORD, ORGANIZE, COGITATE** (think) and **KEEP AT IT.**

Start RIGHT NOW by writing down what you ate earlier today and **R.O.C.K.** it!

---

***Psych Note!*** *I said I'd tell you why it's so important to write things down: No joke, the first reason is that people usually HATE writing a record of what they have eaten so much that MANY people will decide NOT TO EAT A SMALL SNACK OR TREAT just because they know they'll have to write it down!*

---

And writing it down is so annoying to people that many decide the enjoyment they might get from eating a snack is NOT worth the annoyance of having to keep a record of it. So they skip all those little fattening snacks between meals (and ESPECIALLY at night!).

And, as a result, they wind up eating less sugar and fat and wind up . . . losing . . . an . . . extra . . . few . . . pounds . . . a . . . month!

*Congratulations to YOU!*

21

## *T.A.F.N. . . .*

That's **A**ll **F**or **N**ow — Whew, isn't that enough? Whenever you're ready for more, check out the next chapter in this book that interests you.

BUT FIRST! Use the journal forms on the next two pages to help you get started on your RECORD KEEPING.

**Journal Entries** – Copy as often as needed.

8:00 A.M.–10:00 A.M.
   I ate: scrambled eggs, coffee c cream + sugar
       $H_2O$

10:00 A.M.–Noon
   I ate: munchkin, grapes
       turkey sand c tomato, grapes
       $H_2O$

Noon–2:00 P.M.
   I ate:

2:00 P.M.–4:00 P.M.
   I ate:

4:00 P.M.–6:00 P.M.
   I ate:

6:00 P.M.–8:00 P.M.
   I ate:

**Journal Entries** – Copy as often as needed.

8:00 P.M.–10:00 P.M.
   I ate:

10:00 P.M.–Midnight

   I ate:

Midnight–2:00 A.M.
   I ate:

2:00 A.M.–4:00 A.M.
   I ate:

4:00 A.M.–6:00 A.M.
   I ate:

6:00 A.M.–8:00 A.M.
   I ate:

# *NOTES*

*"Suffering occurs from trying to control what is uncontrollable or from neglecting what is within our power."*

*–Epictetus*

# Chapter 3

## Using Power Psychology to Have More Joy in Your Life

### What Is "Power Psychology"?

It is a simple solution to complex personal problems. Psychology is the science of understanding human behavior. Human behavior, of course, is complex and what seems obvious is not always the case. People have been studying — and trying to improve — human behavior since the philosopher Epictetus lectured in the public square of ancient Greece and it is often considered that the European struggle between religion and philosophy was the beginning of modern psychology.

We've come a long way since then and modern science, such as Magnetic Resonance Imaging (MRI), Positron Emission Tomography (PET) and a veritable alphabet soup of other diagnostic assessment tools, has

continued to show that human behavior is caused by "hidden psychological processes." This is just a fancy way of saying, "stuff we do that we usually don't think about very much."

Power Psychology is simply a way of taking what scientists have found out in their laboratories about our "hidden psychological processes" and bringing it OUT of the laboratories and giving it to people in a way they can use in the real world. Why? So people can put "research" to use in their own lives to make real and powerful changes in their own — and others' — behavior to improve the quality of their own lives — and the lives of the people they love. We take these powerful psychological techniques and turn them into **Power Psychology Techniques for Living (PTL)**.

Using **Power Psychology Techniques for Living** can help you change your life for the better. Applying **PTL** to everyday actions and events in your life can improve results in so many areas — health, relationships, income, longevity — the list is probably only limited by your imagination.

This section, Chapter 3 in this book of **Power Psychology Techniques for Living**, focuses upon how you really can have more JOY in your life.

## *When Can I Get Started?*

Right now. There are always only FOUR STEPS to learning a particular set of **PTL**. Each chapter in the **PTL** series is written to be a "stand-alone" chapter, which means that you can read each chapter alone and in any order you wish to learn the particular set of **PTL** that applies to the subject. You don't have to read each chapter starting from the first chapter in the series to the last in order to get a benefit from any chapter.

Each chapter builds on the previous chapters, however, and the more chapters you read, the more **PTL** you can learn to apply in your life. You can learn what you need to know about how you really can have more JOY in your life RIGHT HERE, RIGHT NOW.

This chapter doesn't replace any need for psychological therapy, but it is based on psychological studies about depression, happiness and resilience.

## *How Can Power Psychology Help Me Have More Joy?*

**First,** remember to **P.A.C.E.** yourself. That means, PRACTICE what you learn here; be AWARE of the environment in which you practice; COGITATE (think) about what you are doing; and actually EXPERIENCE the four steps presented here, don't just read them and forget about them! More about the basic **P.A.C.E.** process is discussed in Chapter 1 of this book.

**Second,** understand this: Joy is a conscious, deliberate choice, not an accident. Then, when you are ready, **W.O.R.K.** it out!

**W** – **W**ANT. Like just about anything else in life, you have to **WANT** joy to GET it. Surprisingly, most folks just don't think much about joy or happiness — they're too busy fighting off one disaster, one setback, or one disappointment after another. Sometimes it seems to people like the whole world and stars and planets are all AGAINST them and they are struggling just to stay even and balanced. "Joy? What's joy?," they wonder. "I'm just trying to pay my bills and hope nothing worse happens! Who has time for joy?"

And some other problem ALWAYS will come along, no matter what; it's just a matter of time . . . because LIFE IS JUST LIKE THAT! LIFE CONTAINS PROBLEMS — it always has and it always will. Being sad and unhappy doesn't prevent problems in life and, truly, being happy doesn't prevent problems from happening — problems just happen and as long as the world is spinning, the people living on it will have problems.

---

***Psych Note!*** *It's true — we just CAN'T STOP problems from appearing in our lives any more than we can stop the wind from blowing — it's beyond our control. But we CAN and we OFTEN DO cause our own unhappiness, sadness, misery and depression. That's good news! I know what you're thinking — "Is this guy crazy? HE must need to see a psychologist!" But it IS good news because it clearly illustrates that WE HAVE POWER OVER OUR EMOTIONS! And if we can make ourselves miserable . . . then we can also MAKE OURSELVES HAPPY! That's GOOD NEWS!*

---

It's not you — it's life that generates the problems. BUT how you REACT to the stupid problems that life generates is what's important. And THAT is all up to YOU!

But most people DON'T make themselves happy; they just let themselves get sadder and sadder and more miserable and more hopeless like they've switched on "automatic pilot." They just let themselves sink lower and lower. That can lead to a full-blown CLINICAL DEPRESSION IN AS LITTLE AS 2 WEEKS!

Other psychological problems can also result, such as ANXIETY or PANIC DISORDERS, INSOMNIA, ANGER OUTBURSTS and many other psychological problems! So if you've been feeling really sad, hopeless or miserable for two weeks or longer, it is REALLY a good idea to consult a psychologist or physician for an assessment to be sure that these are not symptoms of a MUCH bigger problem needing psychological treatment.

O – OPTIMISM. Granny used to say, "It's always darkest before the dawn," and she was right. (She also said to take cod liver oil, and it looks like she was right about that, too, but I digress.)

Given the choice between feeling hopeLESS and feeling hopeFUL, which would you choose? HOPEFUL! And it is indeed A CHOICE that we MUST make — a willful, deliberate choice.

After all, who in their right mind would automatically think, "Hey, my basement's flooded. This is great!" Not many people, I'd bet. But even thinking something as odd as that is better and more POSITIVE, HOPEFUL and FORWARD THINKING than thinking, "AW, #%*! Why does everything happen to me?! What did I do to deserve this? I never get a break! I hate this life!!"

Yes, a flooded basement IS a messy, depressing, negative event — that's REALITY. Joyful people, however, ACCEPT reality — they aren't idiots, after all, just joyful — but instead of DWELLING on how horrible something is, joyful people try to focus on how to solve problems. They engage in POSITIVE, not negative, THINKING. As F. Scott Fitzgerald said, "One may see things as hopeless and still be determined to make them otherwise."

And you can TRAIN YOURSELF to think about more positive outcomes to any bad event that's just happened. For example, "What a disaster! I wonder how long it'll take to get this resolved. Who do I have to call? OK, let's get started putting things back together AND MOVE FORWARD."

Notice the difference between a NEGATIVE, hopeLESS mindset that focuses on the bad event ("Oh, NO! I never get a break!") and a more POSITIVE, hopeFUL mindset ("Oh, NO! This is a disaster that I didn't need. Now I have this to deal with, too! Well, OK then, I better get started to get this done and get on with my life.")

Facing a setback? A disaster? YOU CAN DEAL WITH IT — whatever it is — so you have reason to be **OPTIMISTIC.**

**R** – RESILIENCE. **RESILIENCY** is the MINDSET, the ATTITUDE, the BELIEF that — whatever the problem — YOU CAN DEAL WITH IT, RESOLVE IT and move forward with your life. Don't let yourself get bogged down, always thinking how horrible or terrible something is. Yeah, lousy things happen (almost on a daily basis to someone, somewhere) but we need to focus on the SOLUTION, not the PROBLEM.

Keeping your mind focused on the solution — that's **RESILIENCY.** When you keep your mind and your thoughts on the problem or the disaster, that's called CATASTROPHIZING (keeping the disaster alive in your mind) and that even makes it worse because it makes you FEEL worse and worse about what's happened. So focus on **RESILIENCE.** Being knocked down by life isn't news — it happens to everyone! But getting up again, over and over . . . THAT'S the more important thing. That's **RESILIENCY.**

**K** – KEEP AT IT! Deny adversity. Having a bad day? So what? Don't make things worse by being a "Gloomy Gus" and being cranky to family members, co-workers, and poor, innocent waiters, strangers and bus drivers. If something bad or adverse has happened, find a way to think about how you can make the best of it. Like Granny also used to say, "When life gives you lemons, make lemonade!" (OK, Granny could be a bit tiresome, but she had the right idea!)

Is this how you approach setbacks? A) Something lousy just happened and B) It's disrupted your day, so C) You're going to MAKE SURE the rest of your day is ruined by REPEATEDLY thinking about the lousy event over and over again and how bad you feel now!

IT's QUIZ TIME — what's wrong with the above approach? YOU ARE! You are giving yourself over to believing that adversity, having come to visit you today, is going to stay with you all day! Why do that to yourself? Something bad has happened — OK, that stinks. So you're going to make things worse . . . BY FEELING MISERABLE ALL DAY?

I have a better idea: How about figuring out what you can do to make things better if you can; undoing what went wrong if you can; making sure it doesn't happen again if you can; and then MOVING FORWARD onto the next thing you need to do WITHOUT making yourself feel bad about what's happened.

---

*Psych Note!* *Yes, what I'm recommending IS easier said than done. It DOES take practice to get your mind to work this way. But it IS a lot easier than you think once you get started thinking more positively. Don't you have MORE things to do during the day than just dwell on problems? Don't you have work tasks, errands, shopping, whatever? How do you expect to be able to DO those things if your mind is stuck on feeling bad and negative about ONE thing that's happened in the day?*

You owe it to yourself, your family, your co-workers — heck, even to the other cars on the road if you're driving — to keep your mind clear and focused on what you need to be doing RIGHT NOW to avoid creating other problems for yourself. So **DENY adversity** — deal with it as it comes up, but then move on.

## *Your Turn Starts Now!*

**PTL** is about taking what science has learned in the laboratories and putting it to use in your own life, in the real world, starting today. You need to take what you learn from **PTL** and PUT IT INTO PRACTICE IN YOUR LIFE. Don't just THINK about what you've read so far, USE IT, DO IT, PRACTICE IT and do so CONSISTENTLY.

Remember, the more time you spend working on a task, working on it CORRECTLY, that is, the more likely you are to be successful at accomplishing that task. THINKING is very important and is ALWAYS a good place to start any activity, but thinking without ACTION will not change your life very much. It is the EXPERIENCE of putting positive thoughts into positive actions that can improve our quality of life.

**PTL** is a program where you can't lose — you can just win. If you skip or miss a day or make a mistake, just pick up where you left off and keep going forward.

If you've stopped or dropped out of a program — just start again. YOU CAN DO THIS! YES, YOU!

All you need to get started is your brain — and, fortunately, you just happen to have it with you right now! How handy is that? Get that brain working and be willing to **W.O.R.K.** to get more JOY in your life!

**W**ANT IT! **W**ANT more joy and happiness in your life now; be **O**PTIMISTIC, not pessimistic as you go through your day dealing with life events; be **R**ESILIENT when "LIFE" knocks you down — all you need to do is GET BACK UP ("LIFE" really respects that, by the way, and WE also start to RESPECT OURSELVES when that happens). And **K**EEP AT IT. Deny adversity.

One of the granddaddies of positive thinking was Norman Vincent Peale, who famously taught, "Deny the power of adverse conditions!" That is, be optimistic and keep moving forward.

You can START RIGHT NOW to have more joy in your life — so let's get to **W.O.R.K.!**

*T.A.F.N. . . .*

That's **A**ll **F**or **N**ow — Whew, isn't that enough? Whenever you're ready for more, check out the next chapter in this book that interests you.

*BUT FIRST! Start today to put more JOY in your life. Don't wait!*

# *NOTES*

*"Creativity, not money, is used to solve problems."*
*–Robert Rodriguez*

# Chapter 4

## Using Power Psychology to Increase Your Reading Speed in Just One Hour

### What Is "Power Psychology"?

It is a simple solution to complex personal problems. Psychology is the science of understanding human behavior. Human behavior, of course, is complex and what seems obvious is not always the case. People have been studying — and trying to improve — human behavior since the philosopher Epictetus lectured in the public square of ancient Greece and it is often considered that the European struggle between religion and philosophy was the beginning of modern psychology.

We've come a long way since then and modern science, such as Magnetic Resonance Imaging (MRI), Positron Emission Tomography (PET) and a veritable alphabet soup of other diagnostic assessment tools, has continued to show that human behavior is caused by "hidden psychological processes." This is just a fancy way of saying, "stuff we do that we usually don't think about very much."

Power Psychology is simply a way of taking what scientists have found out in their laboratories about our "hidden psychological processes" and bringing it OUT of the laboratories and giving it to people in a way they can use in the real world. Why? So people can put "research" to use in their own lives to make real and powerful changes in their own — and others' — behavior to improve the quality of their own lives — and the lives of the people they love.

We take these powerful scientific psychological techniques and turn them into **Power Psychology Techniques for Living (PTL)**.

Using **Power Psychology Techniques for Living** can help you change your life for the better. Applying **PTL** to everyday actions and events in your life can improve results in so many areas — health, relationships, income, longevity — the list is probably only limited by your imagination.

This section, Chapter 4 in this book of **Power Psychology Techniques for Living**, focuses upon how to use **PTL** to read faster in just one hour.

## *When Can I Get Started?*

Right now. There are always only FOUR STEPS to learning a particular set of **PTL**. Each chapter in the **PTL** series is written to be a "stand-alone" chapter, which means that you can read each chapter alone and in any order you wish to learn the particular set of **PTL** that applies to the subject. You don't have to read each chapter starting from the first chapter in the series to the last in order to get a benefit from any chapter.

Each chapter builds on the previous chapters, however, and the more chapters you read, the more **PTL** you can learn to apply in your life. This chapter doesn't give you a full speed-reading program — it just gives you a taste of what it's like to blaze through novels, magazines and newspapers.

## *How Can Power Psychology Help Me Increase My Reading Speed?*

Remember to **P.A.C.E.** yourself. That means, **PRACTICE** what you learn here; be **AWARE** of the environment in which you practice; **COGITATE** (think) about what you are doing; and actually **EXPERIENCE** the four steps presented here, don't just read them and forget about them! More about the basic **P.A.C.E.** process is discussed in my introductory Power Psychology chapter, Chapter 1 in this book.

Then, when you are **READy**, let's **R.E.A.D.**

**R** – REVIEW what you are going to read. That is, glance through the WHOLE chapter, chapter or section that you are going to read. By doing this, you FAMILIARIZE yourself with what's coming up and get an idea of the layout of the text — length of paragraphs, headings used, spacing and so forth. It's like looking at a general map of where you will be going before you actually start the journey.

Why? Because the biggest "chunk" of reading is understanding what you read and how the author — or publisher — lays out the words on a page. This has a BIG impact on our ability to process the information contained on that page. Ever come across a page that's solid words with no paragraph breaks of any kind? Reading a page like that — let alone SEVERAL pages like that — can be exhausting!

If you aren't prepared for it, you expect a page to be more of a normal layout. When you find that it isn't, it can literally make you NOT want to read it at all. And guess what? If you're REALLY thinking, "I don't want to read this," how much of what you read do you think you will remember? Not much.

---

*Psych Note!* *This technique has a long history in speed-reading literature. It's often called "Surveying," like what map makers do BEFORE they start their maps and what homeowners do before they put up a fence. You really want to know what you're going to be working with BEFORE you start working.*

---

So prepare yourself for what lies ahead — review the material you are going to read BEFORE you start reading. It really does make reading a lot easier and faster.

*And the sneaky part of reviewing what lies ahead?*

You've ALREADY familiarized yourself with some of the content you are going to be reading, so when you actually start READING, it's really more like REVIEWING something you already know a little about!

E – EYES ONLY! Do NOT move your lips or say the words you read inside your head as you read. This habit is VERY COMMON and is called "sub-vocalizing." It means that you aren't just using your eyes to read the words on the page — you are actually silently speaking the words to yourself in your head. (All right, it's true that SOME people REALLY speak the words to themselves out loud or in an audible whisper. That usually attracts the attention of others around the reader who wonder where the voice is coming from and why that reader is whispering to him or herself. Try to not be that kind of reader, OK?)

When you REALLY read — use just your eyes. Run your eyes over the words on the page and try very hard to NOT say the words your eyes see. It's hard in the beginning, but gets easier with practice. Try using your hand or finger as a pointer to keep your eyes following the words on the pages. As you involve your hands in the reading process, you help keep your eyes on track.

And you use the NEXT step to keep your mind OCCUPIED and too busy to SUB-VOCALIZE. See how all this is starting to come together?

**A** – **A**NALYZE what you are reading as you are reading it. Become an ACTIVE reader by asking yourself questions about what you are reading, such as, "How does this build on what I just read a minute ago? Is this an important part of the chapter or just a little sidestep the author took that doesn't seem to really connect with the rest of the story? What does this passage REALLY mean to me?" The more you ask yourself questions the more you keep your mind engaged and aware of what you are reading — and being FOCUSED on what you are reading is the secret to UNDERSTANDING what you read. If you don't understand what you read — if it makes no sense to you — then what have you accomplished? Um . . . nothing?

**D** – **D**ON'T RE-READ! Nope. NEVER. What is there to re-read, anyway? If you have already **R**EVIEWED and kept your **E**YES ON TRACK and **A**NALYZED as you were reading, then what do you hope to gain by reading something TWICE? Did you enjoy it so much you wanted to read it AGAIN? Well, OK, in that case — go ahead!

Generally, though, it's a really BAD IDEA to go back and re-read a passage or sentence because USUALLY your desire to re-read is based on a slight worry that you MISSED something important because you were using this new and uncomfortable reading method. But the odds are — YOU HAVEN'T. Even if you did miss something — what could it have been? Was it a life-changing event? Probably not. It was most probably something related to the story that you were reading and you MOST LIKELY have a really good idea about what that is. Avoid re-reading and don't worry so much about it!

---

*Psych Note!* *We're focusing here on increasing your rate of reading speed for novels, magazine articles and newspapers, don't forget. These types of reading materials usually are NOT very important to remember or absorb with 100% accuracy — usually 70%–80% accuracy is good enough for this type of reading. We are NOT talking about reading legal documents, medical texts and other VITAL or truly IMPORTANT reading material. You CAN speed-read those materials, too, but it takes a LOT more practice than you have now and some EXTRA techniques, but the BASICS that are mentioned here are the backbone of speed-reading those materials, also.*

---

If you want a more structured and in-depth program, search out "speed-reading programs" and chose one that appeals to you. The grandfather (um, grandmother?) of all speed-reading courses is probably the one started by Evelyn Wood, developed decades ago and originally called something like "Reading Dynamics."

But check out complete reading programs if you have an interest and want to build on what you've learned so far.

## *Your Turn Starts Now!*

**PTL** is about taking what science has learned in the laboratories and putting it to use in your own life, in the real world, starting today. You need to take what you learn from **PTL** and PUT IT INTO PRACTICE IN YOUR LIFE. Don't just THINK about what you've read so far — USE IT, DO IT, PRACTICE IT and do so CONSISTENTLY.

Remember, the more time you spend working on a task — working on it CORRECTLY, that is — the more likely you are to be successful at accomplishing that task. THINKING is very important and is ALWAYS a good place to start any activity, but thinking without ACTION will not change your life very much. It is the EXPERIENCE of putting positive thoughts into positive actions that can improve our quality of life.

**PTL** is a program where you can't lose — you can just win. If you skip or miss a day or make a mistake, just pick up where you left off and keep going forward. If you've stopped or dropped out of a program — just start again. YOU CAN DO THIS! YES, YOU!

All you need to get started is your brain — and, fortunately, you just happen to have it with you right now! How handy is that? Get that brain working and **REVIEW**, use your **EYES ONLY**, **ANALYZE** and **DON'T** let yourself re-read.

Just **R.E.A.D.** Practice these techniques and your reading speed will increase in less than an hour.

## *T.A.F.N. . . .*

That's **A**ll **F**or **N**ow — Whew, isn't that enough? Whenever you're ready for more, check out the next chapter in this book that interests you. Until then . . . good **READ**ing!

*BUT FIRST!*

*One last thing . . . A POP QUIZ!*

1. WHAT was the main point of this chapter?

2. WHEN should you survey BEFORE you read?

3. WHY should you ask questions as you read?

4. HOW should your eyes move when reading?

5. WHAT is your name? (OK, that's an EASY one . . . a quick 20 points for you!)

# *NOTES*

# Chapter 5

## *Using Power Psychology to Stop Procrastinating . . .*

### *NOW.*

#### *Helllooo . . .?*

## *What Is "Power Psychology"?*

It is a simple solution to complex personal problems. Psychology is the science of understanding human behavior. Human behavior, of course, is complex and what seems obvious is not always the case. People have been studying — and trying to improve — human behavior since the philosopher Epictetus lectured in the public square of ancient Greece and it is often considered that the European struggle between religion and philosophy was the beginning of modern psychology.

We've come a long way since then and modern science, such as Magnetic Resonance Imaging (MRI), Positron Emission Tomography (PET) and a veritable alphabet soup of other diagnostic assessment tools, has continued to show that human behavior is caused by "hidden psychological processes." This is just a fancy way of saying, "stuff we do that we don't think about very much."

Power Psychology is simply a way of taking what scientists have found out in their laboratories about our "hidden psychological processes" and bringing it OUT of the laboratories and giving it to people in a way they can use in the real world. Why? So people can put "research" to use in their own lives to make real and powerful changes in their own — and others' — behavior to improve the quality of their own lives — and the lives of the people they love.

We take these powerful scientific psychological techniques and turn them into **Power Psychology Techniques for Living (PTL)**.

Using **Power Psychology Techniques for Living** can help you change your life for the better. Applying **PTL** to everyday actions and events in your life can improve results in so many areas — health, relationships, income, longevity — the list is probably only limited by your imagination.

This section, Chapter 5 in this book of **Power Psychology Techniques for Living**, focuses upon how to use **PTL** to STOP PROCRASTINATING. RIGHT NOW.

## When Can I Get Started?

Oh, did I not just say, "Right now?" So, how about RIGHT NOW?! There are always only FOUR STEPS to learning a particular set of **PTL**. Each chapter in the **PTL** series is written to be a "stand-alone" chapter, which means that you can read each chapter alone and in any order you wish to learn the particular set of **PTL** that applies to the subject. You don't have to read each chapter starting from the first chapter in the series to the last to get a benefit from any chapter.

Each chapter builds on the previous chapters, however, and the more chapters you read, the more **PTL** you can learn to apply in your life. This chapter doesn't give you a full review of ALL the possible underlying psychological causes of procrastination, anxiety, delay and putting things off — that's a HUGE area to cover — this chapter just gives you a simple, straightforward action plan to STOP PROCRASTINATING NOW AND GET THINGS DONE! RIGHT NOW.

## How Can Power Psychology Help Me Stop Procrastinating?

Oh, let's talk about that later.

KIDDING! I'm KIDDING, already! Nope. No more procrastinating.

We're getting started NOW!

51

## *Right Now?*

Yes, right now. Scary thought, right? Well, for some people — yes, it is a scary thought! Although some consider "procrastination" as simply the act of replacing high-priority actions with tasks of lower priority, or of skipping unpleasant things in favor of doing something from which one derives enjoyment, such behavior really ISN'T procrastination.

No, skipping things and doing things out of order can be considered merely examples of faulty prioritizing. Procrastination is MUCH different. Procrastination is when you repeatedly put off doing something that you simply MUST get done, but you just DON'T DO IT, despite the (often extreme) consequences or penalties that you then must suffer because of your failure to get the task done when it is due. That's because at the bottom of REAL procrastination, you'll often find FEAR. For some people, it's FEAR OF FAILURE; for others, it's FEAR OF SUCCESS.

But truthfully, WHATEVER the root cause, people who habitually procrastinate are so used to procrastinating that they have simply become used to NOT doing things rather than doing things. In the world of clinical psychology, we'd say that some people have CONDITIONED themselves to procrastinate.

That's just a fancy way of saying that people have LEARNED how to STOP themselves from doing things instead of learning how to START doing things! What? That just doesn't seem to make any sense? Well, believe it or not it's true . . . .

## *Good News, Bad News and Funny News...*

Many, MANY people have simply TAUGHT themselves to procrastinate! But here's the FUNNY thing about it: They don't even KNOW that they have taught themselves to procrastinate — they think it's caused by something or someone else! But no.

We TAUGHT OURSELVES, a long, long time ago, to procrastinate. Then we PRACTICED procrastinating over and over again. And we practiced it PERFECTLY! And we know what PERFECT PRACTICE does for us, don't we? (If not, see my first chapter on Power Psychology and **P.A.C.E.**)

PERFECT PRACTICE MAKES PERFECT! So guess what? Procrastination has now become a HABIT! A very STRONG habit, like smoking cigarettes or eating junk food. It's true that in a very SMALL amount of cases, there MAY BE additional reasons why people procrastinate such as biological addiction to nicotine or biochemical changes due to processed sugar, salt or additives, or even underlying psychological conditions — and I'll explain what to do if you suspect that is the case — but REGARDLESS of how the procrastination might have started, it STILL is a matter of procrastination having become a HABIT.

This is both GOOD and BAD news: BAD news because you created a BAD HABIT and didn't realize it; but awesome GOOD NEWS, because any habit that you have CREATED, you can CHANGE! How great is that?

## *Just R.O.L.L. with It*

First, as always, remember to **P.A.C.E.** yourself. That means, **PRACTICE** what you learn here; be **AWARE** of the environment in which you practice; **COGITATE** (think) about what you are doing; and actually **EXPERIENCE** the four steps presented here, don't just read them and forget about them!

More about the basic **P.A.C.E.** process is discussed in my introductory Power Psychology chapter, Chapter 1 in this book.

Then, when you are ready to stop procrastinating, WHICH, by the way, IS RIGHT NOW, all you need to do next is **R.O.L.L.** into it.

**R** – **R**ELAX, already. Nobody is perfect — and nobody HAS to be perfect. A big reason why many people first learned to procrastinate is because they thought they had to do something PERFECTLY.

But they were wrong — they didn't have to do a task perfectly, especially when first tackling something; all they had to do was just start doing it.

So relax about being perfect, already — nobody is perfect. Not even the people that expect YOU to be "perfect," including your boss, your spouse, your kids, your parents, your siblings, your co-workers or your neighbors!

---

*Psych Note! If you have TROUBLE relaxing, then you need to learn how to RELAX and REDUCE STRESS. Research has shown that relaxation has many, many benefits in reducing stress chemicals in our bodies and in keeping our heads clear and our thinking reasonable. Don't confuse being RELAXED with being LAZY, however.*

---

I use the term RELAXED to mean calm, poised and unflappable — you know, cool under pressure like all those action stars in the movies? NOTHING ever bothers those guys! Or TV doctors in the emergency rooms? That's what I mean by being relaxed . . . calm, cool and in control of your behavior and actions without being nervous.

If you need help learning to remain calm, check out the many resources publicly available or you can check out my **PTL** chapter **"Using Power Psychology to Help Stop Worrying,"** Chapter 10 in this book.

Now, when I say, "being perfect," I MEAN "perfect." As in FLAWLESS. As in "100% exact without ever changing." Ever. I mean absolutely perfect in EVERYTHING, not just really, really good or skilled in SOME things. MANY people are GREAT at what they do and EVERYBODY can do a PERFECT job at something sometimes — just look at the performers in the Olympics who get a "perfect" score in their chosen athletic event. But even THEY aren't ALWAYS totally 100% perfect 100% of the time, in EVERYTHING they do.

That's because it is just not humanly possible to be PERFECTLY PERFECT in everything. It just isn't. Trust me; no matter how PERFECT someone may be in something, they are only average (or maybe even worse!) in most other things. That's just how humans are. Getting a task done well is what humans are built for and always trying to IMPROVE performance is a good aspirational goal. But obsessively seeking perfection in everything? Um . . . probably not a good lifestyle choice. Even diamonds are rated by their flaws, and if NATURE ITSELF isn't perfect in everything, isn't it a little unreasonable to expect humans to be perfect in everything?

O – ORGANIZE what you need to do. If you don't know what you need to do, or don't have all the information or tools needed to complete a project, then why WOULD you try to start something? Knowing what you need to do is the most important part of accomplishing any task; knowing how to do it is the next important aspect. Make sure you know WHAT you need to do and HOW to do it. What if you don't know one or both of those things? Then you've already discovered something important — you procrastinate because you aren't sure of what you need to do! So now that you are aware of that, you know the next step, don't you? That's right — get the information you need to continue.

L – LEARN to ask for what you need from whom you need it. It may be hard at first to ASK someone for what you need, but communication is important to task completion. It's better to ask for instructions, details, clarification — even asking for help is a good idea, if you decide that you need help. Asking for what you need to complete the task is a smart move, because COMMUNICATION and REACHING OUT are important interpersonal skills that show others your commitment and interest in what's going on and how you are expected to be a part of it.

*Psych Note! Communication with others who are affected by your procrastination is SO important, even in small tasks, like not taking out the garbage, cleaning your room, finishing your taxes, and making appointments for your spouse, kids, or parents. Sure, communicating with your colleagues at work is important — DUH — but it's just as important with family members, club members and any other people who are depending on your behavior.*

Don't isolate yourself or be fearful about your procrastination — communicate with others about what you need to complete your task. It'll help them realize what roles THEY might be playing in delays that they usually may attribute to you.

L – LET it flow, already! Once you've gotten all the information you need and have assembled the tools or resources necessary, then just get the process started. Don't forget; procrastination is the habit of putting things off until tomorrow ("crastinus" is of Latin derivation meaning "of to-morrow" and plain ol' "cras" just means "to-morrow"). So don't PRO-crastinate, ANTI-crastinate! Be different from everyone else — become an ANTICRATE. (T-shirts, anyone?)

---

*Psych Note! It's been said, "Perfection is the opposite of progress." It's also the enemy of task completion. But I said I'd tell you what to do if you suspect that you may have an underlying clinical or psychological condition that makes overcoming procrastination more difficult and here it is:*

*If you have ANXIETY, DEPRESSION, a LEARNING DISABILITY, or perhaps ATTENTION DEFICIT HYPERACTIVITY DISORDER (ADHD) — and many, many people DO have these conditions and do not know it — you should strongly consider consulting an experienced behavioral psychologist for a quick assessment and more specific remediation, if needed.*

---

WAIT! Who said anything about medication? I didn't say anything about medication, did I? No; typically, the treatment for the common behavioral problems noted above is a behavioral treatment or a cognitive-behavioral treatment package done by an experienced behavioral clinician.

And YES, sometimes — SOMETIMES — medication may be a part of an effective treatment program, but trust me: Pills won't make you stop procrastinating; learning how to change your behavior will.

Sadly, however, your local PCP (we used to call them "doctors," remember?) may not know enough about these conditions to be able to diagnose them appropriately, let alone properly treat them, depending on what part of the country you live in and what access you have to health care, but it surely couldn't hurt to start a conversation about this with him or her.

Typically, however, it's a behavioral psychologist who is the go-to expert in the behavioral treatment of such matters. So don't be shy about asking for a second opinion. But, since you may not have a behavioral psychologist located close by, start by asking any licensed health care professional for a first opinion or an appropriate referral. When in doubt — CHECK IT OUT!

## *Your Turn Starts Now!*

**PTL** is about taking what science has learned in the laboratories and putting it to use in your own life, in the real world, starting today. You need to take what you learn from **PTL** and PUT IT INTO PRACTICE IN YOUR LIFE. Don't just THINK about what you've read so far. USE IT, DO IT, PRACTICE IT and do so CONSISTENTLY.

Remember, the more time you spend working on a task — working on it CORRECTLY, that is — the more likely you are to be successful at accomplishing that task. THINKING is very important and is ALWAYS a good place to start any activity, but thinking without ACTION will not change your life very much. It is the EXPERIENCE of putting positive thoughts into positive actions that can improve our quality of life.

**PTL** is a program where you can't lose — you can just win. If you skip or miss a day or make a mistake, just pick up where you left off and keep going forward. If you've stopped or dropped out of a program — just start again. YOU CAN DO THIS! YES, YOU!

All you need to get started is your brain — and, fortunately, you just happen to have it with you right now! How handy is that?

Get that brain working and **R**ELAX already; **O**RGANIZE what you need; **L**EARN to ask for needed help and then **L**ET IT FLOW.

Practice these techniques and you'll soon develop a NEW habit — a SUCCESS HABIT.

## *T.A.F.N.* . . .

That's **A**ll **F**or **N**ow — Whew, isn't that enough? Whenever you're ready for more, check out the next chapter in this book that interests you. Until then . . . get **ROLL**ing!

# *NOTES*

*"I figure practice puts your brains in your muscles."*

*–Sam Snead*

# Chapter 6

## Using Power Psychology to Turbocharge Your Abs Workout

### What Is "Power Psychology"?

It is a simple solution to complex personal problems. Psychology is the science of understanding human behavior. Human behavior, of course, is complex and what seems obvious is not always the case. People have been studying — and trying to improve — human behavior since the philosopher Epictetus lectured in the public square of ancient Greece and it is often considered that the European struggle between religion and philosophy was the beginning of modern psychology.

We've come a long way since then and modern science, such as Magnetic Resonance Imaging (MRI), Positron Emission Tomography (PET) and a veritable alphabet soup of other diagnostic assessment tools, has continued to show that human behavior is caused by "hidden psychological processes." This is just a fancy way of saying, "stuff we do that we usually don't think about very much."

Power Psychology is simply a way of taking what scientists have found out in their laboratories about our "hidden psychological processes" and bringing it OUT of the laboratories and giving it to people in a way they can use in the real world. Why? So people can put "research" to use in their own lives to make real and powerful changes in their own — and others' — behavior to improve the quality of their own lives — and the lives of the people they love.

We take these powerful scientific psychological techniques and turn them into **Power Psychology Techniques for Living (PTL)**.

Using **Power Psychology Techniques for Living** can help you change your life for the better. Applying **PTL** to everyday actions and events in your life can improve results in so many areas — health, relationships, income, longevity — the list is probably only limited by your imagination.

This section, Chapter 6 in this book of **Power Psychology Techniques for Living**, focuses upon how to use **PTL** to turbocharge your abs workout — well, ANY physical workout, actually.

## *When Can I Get Started?*

Right now. There are always only FOUR STEPS to learning a particular set of **PTL**. Each chapter in the **PTL** series is written to be a "stand-alone" chapter, which means that you can read each chapter alone and in any order you wish to learn the particular set of **PTL** that applies to the subject. You don't have to read each chapter starting from the first chapter in the series to the last in order to get a benefit from any chapter.

Each chapter builds on the previous chapters, however, and the more chapters you read, the more **PTL** you can learn to apply in your life. This chapter doesn't give you a full exercise or workout program, because I expect you already have one that you use. This chapter just gives you a simple, straightforward action plan to improve the results of your physical workout — RIGHT NOW.

## *How Can Power Psychology Help Me with My Abs Workout?*

First, as always, remember to **P.A.C.E.** yourself. That means, **PRACTICE** what you learn here; be **AWARE** of the environment in which you practice; **COGITATE** (think) about what you are doing; and actually **EXPERIENCE** the four steps presented here, don't just read them and forget about them!

More about the basic **P.A.C.E.** process is discussed in my introductory Power Psychology chapter,

Chapter 1 in this book. Then, when you are ready to get more from your abs — or ANY workout — all you need to do next is throw the **D.I.C.E.**

**D – D**IETARY awareness is REALLY important. Notice your diet. There are many diets available, of course, and mostly it is those "weight LOSS diets" that get all the publicity. But "diet" simply refers to what you eat on a daily basis. The psychological aspects of weight loss, weight maintenance diets, and dieting are too lengthy to review here, but I do write about **PTL** for weight loss in a separate Power Psychology chapter called **"Using Power Psychology to Drop Up to 6 Pounds"** in Chapter 2 of this book.

---

*Psych Note!* Always check with your doctor before making any changes in your diet, exercise and food intake routines.

---

You already have a diet, of course — it's whatever you put into your body on a regular basis! But is it healthy? Does it contain hidden sugar, saturated fats and salt? If so, then your own diet is working against your own abs workout.

The first step in turbocharging your regular abs work-out is to examine your diet to make sure you aren't working hard during your abs work-out and then undoing all that hard work every time you feed yourself.

*Psych Note!* *If you aren't sure which everyday diet makes sense for most people, then I recommend you check out the Mediterranean Diet or the D.A.S.H. Diet. You can find information about both of those diets on the Internet and through the US National Institute of Health websites. And drink LOTS of water unless your doctor advises you otherwise.*

**I** – IMAGINE that! You have to start using your imagination. That is, you have to VISUALIZE the abs workout you are using. PICTURE yourself doing your abs workout CORRECTLY and PERFECTLY when you ARE and, more importantly, when you ARE NOT actually performing your abs workout. Going to work on the bus, train or subway? PICTURE yourself doing your abs workout instead of reading the newspaper or reading your book.

Waiting for dinner to cook? PICTURE yourself performing your abs workout CORRECTLY and PERFECTLY instead of watching the news or listening to the radio.

*Psych Note!* *Athletes and sports psychologists have known for years that PRACTICING ATHLETIC PERFORMANCES IN YOUR HEAD has a positive and beneficial impact on an athlete's real performance. Ever seen basketball players or golfers take a practice jump shot or putt WITHOUT using a ball? I have. They do it to put a good psych image of a perfect shot in their head or to erase the image of a bad shot they have just made. Professional athletes know the VALUE of visualization. Now, so do you!*

Waiting in line? PICTURE yourself doing your PERFECT abs workout instead of getting frustrated or angry. All this IMAGINARY practice actually has a beneficial effect on your ACTUAL abs workout.

C – COGITATE. Well, this is a twenty-five cent word that I like to use that really just means "think." (So what good is having a Ph.D. if you can't use a few fancy words now and then?) We DO know from psychological research that life-long learning and always learning new things is the best way to ward off age-related memory loss and other poor thinking conditions.

More importantly, by THINKING about how to do your abs workout CORRECTLY and PERFECTLY over and over again, you will likely find that you actually ARE doing your abs workout better and better each time you work out!

---

***Psych Note!*** *Thinking is really important. What we think provides the FUEL for our behaviors. The more you THINK about improving your abs workout, the better you will get at it and the more efficiently you will perform. Also, research has indicated that simply THINKING about a physical exercise actually causes very, very slight, but still measurable, changes in muscle development! Now who would have believed that? But it's true. No, you can't just sit on the couch and just think about exercising — thinking doesn't cause THAT much muscle change — but it sure will help you when you get to the gym!*

---

E – EXPERIENCE. **PTL** is about taking what science has learned in the laboratories and putting it to use in your own life, in the real world, starting today. You need to take what you learn from **PTL** and PUT IT INTO PRACTICE IN YOUR LIFE. Don't just cogitate, I mean, don't just THINK about what you've read so far, put it into practice.

THINKING is very important and is ALWAYS a good place to start an activity, but thinking without ACTION will not change your life very much. It is the EXPERIENCE of putting our thoughts into action that improves our quality of life.

*Psych Note!* Where do you want **PTL** to take you today? Your ability to improve areas of your life is usually limited by a lack of goals, dreams or desires. Make **PTL** an everyday part of your life for improvement in many little areas as well as big ones. Put **PTL** to the test. It can't hurt to try, can it? Life is experiential, not simply observational. So let's get started: Right here. Right now. The next section is your first lesson.

## HA! Mule . . .

You WILL need your brain for this next exercise — and, fortunately, you just happen to have it with you right now! How handy is that? Get that brain working: Let's move it, move it, MOVE IT, gym rat!

OK: Put yourself in a comfortable position for the next five minutes where you won't be disturbed and close your eyes — or leave them open, it's all a matter of personal choice — and just DAYDREAM about yourself doing your abs workout.

SEE your regular workout area, SEE yourself going through your regular routine and PICTURE yourself performing the routine CORRECTLY and PERFECTLY. If you picture yourself making a mistake, immediately PICTURE yourself DOING IT CORRECTLY.

---

*Psych Note!* Don't be discouraged if the first few times you try this it is more difficult than you expected — when you first start visualizing, it takes a while for your brain to get used to it. Practice in five-minute segments 4–5 times a day and it will get easier and easier. Just start practicing and don't quit.

---

## *Your Turn Starts Now!*

**PTL** is about taking what science has learned in the laboratories and putting it to use in your own life, in the real world, starting today. You need to take what you learn from **PTL** and PUT IT INTO PRACTICE IN YOUR LIFE. Don't just THINK about what you have read so far — USE IT, DO IT, PRACTICE IT and do so CONSISTENTLY.

Remember, the more time you spend working on a task — working on it CORRECTLY, that is, the more likely you are to be successful at accomplishing that task. THINKING is very important and is ALWAYS a good place to start any activity, but thinking without ACTION will not change your life very much.

It is the EXPERIENCE of putting positive thoughts into positive actions that can improve our quality of life.

**PTL** is a program where you can't lose — you can just win. If you skip or miss a day or make a mistake, just pick up where you left off and keep going forward. If you've stopped or dropped out of a program — just start again. YOU CAN DO THIS! YES, YOU!

And, as always, all you need to get started is your brain — and, as you proved a few minutes ago, you still happen to have it with you! SO let's get that brain working AGAIN and pay attention to your DIET; IMAGINE the best workout ever; COGITATE about how perfectly you are doing that workout; and actually EXPERIENCE that perfect workout in your imagination AND in real life!

## *T.A.F.N. . . .*

That's **A**ll **F**or **N**ow — Whew, isn't that enough? Whenever you're ready for more, check out the next chapter in this book that interests you. Until then . . . throw those **D.I.C.E.!**

# *NOTES*

# Chapter 7

## Using Power Psychology to Help Improve Your Child's Grades This Quarter

### What Is "Power Psychology"?

It is a simple solution to complex personal problems. Psychology is the science of understanding human behavior. Human behavior, of course, is complex and what seems obvious is not always the case. People have been studying — and trying to improve — human behavior since the philosopher Epictetus lectured in the public square of ancient Greece and it is often considered that the European struggle between religion and philosophy was the beginning of modern psychology.

We've come a long way since then and modern science, such as Magnetic Resonance Imaging (MRI), Positron Emission Tomography (PET) and a veritable alphabet soup of other diagnostic assessment tools, has continued to show that human behavior is caused by "hidden psychological processes." This is just a fancy way of saying, "stuff we do that we usually don't think about very much."

Power Psychology is simply a way of taking what scientists have found out in their laboratories about our "hidden psychological processes" and bringing it OUT of the laboratories and giving it to people in a way they can use in the real world. Why? So people can put "research" to use in their own lives to make real and powerful changes in their own — and others' — behavior to improve the quality of their own lives — and the lives of the people they love.

We take these powerful scientific psychological techniques and turn them into **Power Psychology Techniques for Living (PTL)**.

Using **Power Psychology Techniques for Living** can help you change your life for the better. Applying **PTL** to everyday actions and events in your life can improve results in so many areas — health, relationships, income, longevity — the list is probably only limited by your imagination.

This section, Chapter 7 in this book of **Power Psychology Techniques for Living**, focuses upon how to use **PTL** to help improve your child's grades in school, especially grade school and middle school.

## *When Can I Get Started?*

Right now. There are always only FOUR STEPS to learning a particular set of **PTL**. Each chapter in the **PTL** series is written to be a "stand-alone" chapter, which means that you can read each chapter alone and in any order you wish to learn the particular set of **PTL** that applies to the subject. You don't have to read each chapter starting from the first in the series to the last to get a benefit from any chapter.

Each chapter builds on the previous chapters, however, and the more chapters you read, the more **PTL** you can learn to apply in your life. This chapter doesn't give you a full "How to Study" program, because I expect you already have one that you use. This chapter will help fill in some gaps in the program that you are using and just gives you a simple, straightforward action plan to improve your child's grades — RIGHT NOW.

Of course, if you need a full study program, you can consult my book, *TEN LESSONS in How to Study Using Power Psychology Techniques* or other, similar study books.

## *How Can Power Psychology Help Me Improve My Child's Grades?*

First, as always, remember to **P.A.C.E.** yourself. That means, **P**RACTICE what you learn here; be **A**WARE of the environment in which you practice; **C**OGITATE (think) about what you are doing; and actually EXPERIENCE the four steps presented here, don't just read them and forget about them! More about the basic **P.A.C.E.** process is discussed in my introductory Power Psychology chapter, Chapter 1 in this book.

Then, when you are ready to help your child improve his or her grades, the rest is a **S.N.A.P.!**

## So Let's S.N.A.P. to It!

**S** – SUPPORT your child's HOMEWORK routine! Make sure your child has a space in the house that is set aside for her or him to actually DO THEIR HOMEWORK. You'd be surprised how few kids have a regular time and area set aside for them to get their homework done. This is a small and easy detail that most parents, believe it or not, fail to arrange for their children. Set aside a particular time and area for the homework to be done.

Also, make sure it is QUIET for your favorite student to CONCENTRATE and FOCUS on what he or she must read or think about it. NOISE IS VERY DISTRACTING to brains that are trying to concentrate — well, yes; it's also distracting to, ahem, older brains — no offense, Moms and Dads. Really, get your kid's homework organized by starting out with a set time and space especially for homework completion.

This indicates to your child how IMPORTANT parents think homework is.

*Psych Note!* *Homework can account for as much as 60% of a student's overall grade and if the student is having academic trouble in class because of medical absences, poor test grades or similar classroom work difficulties, good ol' fashioned HOMEWORK completion is what many schools often look to as an indication of curriculum accomplishment and performance. This is especially true if there are PROJECTS or other OUT OF CLASS assignments that have been made — if your kid misses many of these (and sometimes even only a few of them!) there will be NO WAY to make them up in class or after the deadline has passed.*

**N** - NO YELLING! (This means YOU, Dad and/or Mom.) What's that? You never yell? Ah, yes you DO yell — but here's the tricky part. While most parents DON'T THINK that they yell at their kids — most kids THINK THEY DO! How can that be? Simple — kids have a different definition of "yelling."

To KIDS, "yelling" can include a parent using a stern voice, a certain TONE of voice, an ATTITUDE that the parent has and, sometimes, even the words that are used — even if there is no increase in loudness. To PARENTS, of course, yelling is . . . YELLING!

But not to kids. So take note: No Yelling. If in doubt, ask the expert — your kid! Just ask, "Um, does it sometimes sound as though I'm yelling at you about your homework?"

And kindly resist the impulse to yell back, "NO, I'M NOT! *THIS* IS YELLING!" no matter how humorous you think that would be . . . it won't bring a chuckle to your kid, funny man . . . .

**A** – ACTIVELY participate in your child's homework! How well is your kid doing with homework and academic assignments in general? You'd be surprised how many parents do not take the time to even be informed about what homework actually IS DUE — let alone try to HELP their kids with it. Many schools now are adopting — slowly, very slowly — websites that let parents check on what homework has been assigned.

Even then, some teachers forget or don't have enough time to put the assignments on the website! But be aware of what the homework is for your child in EVERY subject. In this ONE area, however, DO NOT ask the "expert" (that is, your kid) what their homework is. Very often, the child is clueless about the assignment or just might want to skip it all together, which is REALLY hard to do if the parent already knows what homework has been assigned.

So avoid a possible trouble area and talk to the teacher about how you, the parent, can ALWAYS know what that teacher, and every teacher, has assigned for homework. And, while we're on the subject, ALWAYS NOTICE how your child is doing with their homework. Seek teacher-parent conferences and look at the work your child brings home and review it.

In general, take an interest in what your child is doing in school and especially notice their homework. When you take the time with your child and show an interest in what they are doing, just by showing some POSITIVE attention (that means, ahem, NO YELLING, see above, Dads) a kid's self-esteem can really improve and so can their effort. Teachers will also notice your involvement and MOST teachers may be very happy to have a parent who actively supports what the teacher is trying to do in the classroom.

*Psych Note! Most teachers — but, sadly, NOT ALL teachers. Surprisingly enough, there may be MANY teachers who will not like the parent "interfering" with the child's school and learning behavior. "It's the child's responsibility," the teacher may say. "They need to learn to be responsible without someone looking over their shoulder." In other words, the teacher is telling you to "butt out" of an important part of your kid's development. Don't buy into such nonsense. By paying attention to what your kid's homework assignments are, you are ALSO keeping tabs on how the teacher and school are preparing your child (or NOT preparing your child) for the next grade and for his or her future LIFE!*

Let's not forget, PARENTS are the GATEKEEPERS for their child's future. YOU need to SUPERVISE your child's academic development and behavior just the same way you must supervise your child's overall development and behavior out of school.

Can you imagine a POLICE OFFICER or a JUDGE saying to a parent, "Stop interfering. This is the child's responsibility. They need to learn to be responsible without someone looking over their shoulder. We'll take care of things, OK?" YIKES!

**P** – **P**OWER up your kid's homework performance! No, I'm not telling you to do your kid's homework WITH them — you probably couldn't keep up, anyway! No; what I'm saying is to use your knowledge as a parent who has taken NOTICE of what the homework is and is SUPPORTING your kid's best efforts to complete his or her homework and who has also TALKED to the teachers about the homework and academic expectations.

If you CAN, then HELP your child as the child does the homework, but don't do the homework for the child. If you CAN'T HELP — and MANY parents just can't help their kid with homework because the parent or child gets too frustrated or tearful or there is too much yelling — then just FIND SOMEONE ELSE who CAN help your child and get that person to HELP YOUR CHILD with the homework.

This is easier than you may think — an uncle, an aunt, an older student from the high school or college, extra help from the school — all these ways are possible and advisable.

DO NOT let your child struggle with homework or academic work: GET HELP and get it SOONER, not later.

If you don't know how to start, ask your school. (If your school is not helpful — and believe me, LOTS of schools aren't — you can get some more information from my newsletter article **"What to Do When Your Child and Teacher Don't Get Along."**

You can sign up for the newsletter — it's FREE, by the way — at: www.TotalSchoolSuccess.com.

---

*Psych Note! Homework is where most of the learning gets done, after all, because ALL LEARNING IS SELF-LEARNING! Teachers can either HELP students learn (that is, make it easier for them) or HINDER students from learning (that is, make it harder for them) simply by the way they organize and present things to a student or a class, but in order to truly LEARN anything (that is, to really UNDERSTAND and KNOW something) we all have to "get it" somehow and make it ours. We must POSSESS knowledge, we must OWN it, much as we own a car or a book or DVDs.*

---

If we do not UNDERSTAND something, then we do not have "knowledge," we simply have "information." And information without understanding is no better than a book that has never been read, a friend that you never see, a life that you never truly live.

## Your Turn Starts Now!

**PTL** is about taking what science has learned in the laboratories and putting it to use in your own life, in the real world, starting today. You need to take what you learn from **PTL** and PUT IT INTO PRACTICE IN YOUR LIFE. Don't just THINK about what you've read so far, USE IT, DO IT, PRACTICE IT and do so CONSISTENTLY.

Remember, the more time you spend working on a task — working on it CORRECTLY, that is — the more likely you are to be successful at accomplishing that task. THINKING is very important and is ALWAYS a good place to start any activity, but thinking without ACTION will not change your life very much.

It is the EXPERIENCE of putting positive thoughts into positive actions that improves our quality of life.

**PTL** is a program where you can't lose — you can just win. If you skip or miss a day or make a mistake, just pick up where you left off and keep going forward. If you've stopped or dropped out of a program — just start again. YOU CAN DO THIS! YES, YOU!

And, as always, all you need to get started is your brain — and, you probably still happen to have it with you if you've read this far.

SUPPORT your kid's homework efforts; and **NO** YELLING as you do so! ACTIVELY participate in your child's educational process and **P**OWER UP your kid's performance by paying attention to when they are struggling and GETTING HELP for them SOONER, NOT LATER.

## T.A.F.N. . . .

That's **A**ll **F**or **N**ow — Whew, isn't that enough? Whenever you're ready for more, check out the next chapter in this book that interests you. Until then, help your child improve their grades RIGHT NOW by getting in touch with the teacher!

*It's a S.N.A.P.*

# *NOTES*

# Chapter 8

## *Using Power Psychology to Help Improve Your Work Relationships*

### *What Is "Power Psychology"?*

It is a simple solution to complex personal problems. Psychology is the science of understanding human behavior. Human behavior, of course, is complex and what seems obvious is not always the case. People have been studying — and trying to improve — human behavior since the philosopher Epictetus lectured in the public square of ancient Greece and it is often considered that the European struggle between religion and philosophy was the beginning of modern psychology.

We've come a long way since then and modern science, such as Magnetic Resonance Imaging (MRI), Positron Emission Tomography (PET) and a veritable alphabet soup of other diagnostic assessment tools, has

continued to show that human behavior is caused by "hidden psychological processes." This is just a fancy way of saying, "stuff we do that we usually don't think about very much."

Power Psychology is simply a way of taking what scientists have found out in their laboratories about our "hidden psychological processes" and bringing it OUT of the laboratories and giving it to people in a way they can use in the real world. Why? So people can put "research" to use in their own lives to make real and powerful changes in their own — and others' — behavior to improve the quality of their own lives — and the lives of the people they love.

We take these powerful scientific psychological techniques and turn them into **Power Psychology Techniques for Living (PTL)**.

Using **Power Psychology Techniques for Living** can help you change your life for the better. Applying **PTL** to everyday actions and events in your life can improve results in so many areas — health, relationships, income, longevity — the list is probably only limited by your imagination.

This section, Chapter 8 in this book of **Power Psychology Techniques for Living**, focuses upon how to use **PTL** to help improve your work relationships and your job performance.

## When Can I Get Started?

Right now. There are always only FOUR STEPS to learning a particular set of **PTL**. Each chapter in the **PTL** series is written to be a "stand-alone" chapter, which means that you can read each chapter alone and in any order you wish to learn the particular set of **PTL** that applies to the subject.

You don't have to read each chapter starting from the first chapter in the series to the last to get a benefit from any chapter.

Each chapter builds on the previous chapters, however, and the more chapters you read, the more **PTL** you can learn to apply in your life. This chapter doesn't tell you EVERYTHING you need to know about being a success on the job, or about finding the right job for you or about dealing with an abusive boss or bullying coworkers — and remember that there ARE books or coaches available to help you deal with such events — this chapter will help provide you with tips on how to improve your job experience and deal with a workplace environment that may possibly be less than ideal for you — RIGHT NOW.

## How Can Power Psychology Help Me Improve My Work Relationships?

First, as always, remember to **P.A.C.E.** yourself. That means, **PRACTICE** what you learn here; be **AWARE** of the environment in which you practice;

COGITATE (think) about what you are doing; and actually EXPERIENCE the four steps presented here, don't just read them and forget about them!

## *Have a Job? B.R.A.G. About It!*

More about the basic **P.A.C.E.** process is discussed in my introductory Power Psychology chapter, Chapter 1 in this book.

Then, when you are ready to improve your work relationships and job experience, just get ready, set and **B.R.A.G.!** Think your job is nothing to brag about? Think again!

**B** – BE QUIET, already. Most work relationships start to go downhill because of political differences, religious differences, child-rearing differences, attitude differences — in short, EVERYTHING except work differences.

Most people view work as a SOCIAL experience, not a money-making experience, that is, they think WORK is like HIGH SCHOOL and most students went to high school for the social experience of being with their friends, NOT to learn academics. They thought school was for SOCIALIZING. (Here's the memo: It wasn't.)

Although MOST WORKERS ACT like high school students (yes, in some cases, they act like JUNIOR high school students, not adult workers), work is about MAKING MONEY for yourself, but, MORE

IMPORTANTLY, making money for the company. It is also about making your boss LOOK GOOD (or at the very least not making the boss look bad!).

So how do you do that? Simple. You go to work and just DO THE WORK, first and foremost. STICK TO YOUR JOB and keep yourself POLITE, FRIENDLY and PLEASANT at work, but DO NOT talk about others, take sides or FORCE your own ideas and opinions on others.

RESIST the impulse to view the workplace as your SOCIAL OUTLET or, even worse, like it was a FAMILY! It's not — your family can't fire you, ruin your chances at a better job, or hopelessly demoralize you and crush your soul, despite their threats to do so.

*Psych Note!* *OK, some families actually CAN do that to you — but you can always leave the TRAUMA resulting from such a family behind and make a new life for yourself — especially with the help of a really good THERAPIST. You can also leave a job where the boss is ruining your self-esteem, productivity and sucking the life out of you, and you MIGHT even be able to sue the boss and company, too.*

But this isn't a chapter about what to do when the bricks hit the wall — it's an example of how to use **Power Psychology Techniques** to IMPROVE WORK RELATIONSHIPS so none of that happens to you. And AVOIDING dire work situations is much better than REPAIRING yourself after them, isn't it?

**R** – **R**ELATE APPROPRIATELY. Keeping to yourself doesn't mean becoming a hermit, never talking to anyone about anything — although some workers are like that! Probably they are like that to avoid any problems — not a bad move, but it is usually better to be a functioning human being at work than to just never speak to anyone.

But what is the best way to keep yourself free from all the silly high school, um, I mean, workplace cliques, sideshows and intrigues? Just keep remembering that you are not at your friends' house, your therapist's or doctor's office, or your church confessional.

Ask yourself: "If I was at a party where I didn't know anyone and a stranger came up to me and asked me what my co-worker just asked me, how would I respond?" Chances are, you probably WOULDN'T answer by telling your life story or revealing all your prejudices. And you wouldn't — shouldn't — assume that the person you are speaking to thinks just like you do. So respond to others and relate to them the way you would do if you were on a subway or on the street — CAREFULLY and THOUGHTFULLY, not carelessly.

**A** – **A**WARENESS of others' SENSITIVITIES. Yes: Work is not a live FACEBOOK event, but IT IS a place where EVERYTHING you say and do is put on the wall for EVERYONE TO SEE AND COMMENT ON.

And it never is taken down. Ever. And you can't effectively or efficiently fight it, either. SO AVOID IT. You do that by thinking, "How could I possibly

say something that might offend this person —
especially since I don't know what they deeply
believe or what is truly important to them?" Answer:
"YOU DON'T KNOW FOR SURE, DO YOU?" So
answer accordingly.

Some good answers: "Wow, I just don't know about
that. Sounds interesting, though, doesn't it?" Or,
when confronted with a bold statement, try, "Is it?"
Or perhaps, "Does it?" Play around with some
neutral sounding, but responsive, answers to see
what you come up with. Try them out on some REAL
friends, away from work, to see how they sound.
After all, that's what kids do in junior high.

---

*Psych Note! Examples of thoughtless answers are
everywhere, if you just pay attention. A tenant once asked
his landlord, who was a lawyer, what the best way was to
repair a broken window. The landlord was just about to
answer, then stopped and said, "I really don't know. Did
you break a window in the house?"*

*And we all know the story about an employee at a
company party who was at the punch bowl,
complaining about his boss to a young woman he
didn't know. "Oh," she responded, "You mean my
Dad?" Not good.*

---

G – GET A LIFE. OK, this is not as obvious as it
may seem. Many people REALLY DO look upon
their job as their main social outlet. And it's hard for
them to find OTHER social outlets, but people really
need to — it's important to keep your work and

social lives distinct and separate — for your own sanity and for the opportunity to do good work AND THEN LEAVE WORK AT WORK.

We seem to live in a time where people are encouraged to never LEAVE WORK BEHIND, where work is everything and the most important element in one's life. Don't believe it. Don't believe it at all. Don't live to work — just work to help you live a better life.

## *Your Turn Starts Now!*

**PTL** is about taking what science has learned in the laboratories and putting it to use in your own life, in the real world, starting today. You need to take what you learn from **PTL** and PUT IT INTO PRACTICE IN YOUR LIFE.

Don't just THINK about what you've read so far — USE IT, DO IT, PRACTICE IT and do so CONSISTENTLY.

Remember, the more time you spend working on a task — working on it CORRECTLY, that is— the more likely you are to be successful at accomplishing that task. THINKING is very important and is ALWAYS a good place to start any activity, but thinking without ACTION will not change your life very much.

It is the EXPERIENCE of putting positive thoughts into positive actions that can improve our quality of life.

**PTL** is a program where you can't lose — you can just win. If you skip or miss a day or make a mistake, just pick up where you left off and keep going forward. If you've stopped or dropped out of a program — just start again. YOU CAN DO THIS! YES, YOU!

And, as always, all you need to get started is your brain — and you just happen to have it with you RIGHT NOW. How handy is that? So then resolve to USE IT to **BE QUIET AT WORK.**

Don't try to be the life of the workplace — leave that for someone else to do and good luck to them; maybe they are really good at it and why do you want to challenge them?

**R**ESPOND respectfully and appropriately, being careful and thoughtful not to even accidentally offend someone.

Be **A**WARE of what's going on around you at work, but don't let yourself get sucked into one side or another of office politics or favoritism. You are there to do your job — you are a neutral party, not a follower. Believe me, your boss and co-workers will notice and respect you for it.

And **GET A LIFE** outside of work: It could be the smartest work-related decision you've ever made!

## *T.A.F.N. . . .*

That's **A**ll **F**or **N**ow — Whew, isn't that enough? Whenever you're ready for more, check out the next chapter in this book that interests you.

Until then, understand that YOUR job really is something to **B.R.A.G.** about!

# *NOTES*

*"Failure is not fatal; it is the courage to continue that counts."*
*–Winston Churchill*

# Chapter 9

## *Using Power Psychology to Help Improve the Quality of Your Sleep*

### *What Is "Power Psychology"?*

It is a simple solution to complex personal problems. Psychology is the science of understanding human behavior. Human behavior, of course, is complex and what seems obvious is not always the case. People have been studying — and trying to improve — human behavior since the philosopher Epictetus lectured in the public square of ancient Greece and it is often considered that the European struggle between religion and philosophy was the beginning of modern psychology.

We've come a long way since then and modern science, such as Magnetic Resonance Imaging (MRI), Positron Emission Tomography (PET) and a veritable alphabet soup of other diagnostic assessment tools, has

continued to show that human behavior is caused by "hidden psychological processes." This is just a fancy way of saying, "stuff we do that we usually don't think about very much."

Power Psychology is simply a way of taking what scientists have found out in their laboratories about our "hidden psychological processes" and bringing it OUT of the laboratories and giving it to people in a way they can use in the real world. Why? So people can put "research" to use in their own lives to make real and powerful changes in their own — and others' — behavior to improve the quality of their own lives — and the lives of the people they love.

We take these powerful scientific psychological techniques and turn them into **Power Psychology Techniques for Living (PTL)**.

Using **Power Psychology Techniques for Living** can help you change your life for the better. Applying **PTL** to everyday actions and events in your life can improve results in so many areas — health, relationships, income, longevity — the list is probably only limited by your imagination.

This section, Chapter 9 in this book of **Power Psychology Techniques for Living**, focuses upon how to use **PTL** to help improve the quality of your sleep.

## When Can I Get Started?

Right now. There are always only FOUR STEPS to learning a particular set of **PTL**. Each chapter in the **PTL** series is written to be a "stand-alone" chapter, which means that you can read each chapter alone and in any order you wish to learn the particular set of **PTL** that applies to the subject. You don't have to read each chapter starting from the first chapter in the series to the last in order to get a benefit from any chapter.

Each chapter builds on the previous chapters, however, and the more chapters you read, the more **PTL** you can learn to apply in your life. This chapter doesn't tell you EVERYTHING you need to know about sleep disorders, sleep treatments or how to get a sleep study done by your physician — but it DOES give you the basics of what is called "sleep hygiene" to help you improve the quality of your sleep right now.

## How Can Power Psychology Help Me Improve My Quality of Sleep?

First, as always, remember to **P.A.C.E.** yourself. That means, PRACTICE what you learn here; be AWARE of the environment in which you practice; COGITATE (think) about what you are doing; and actually EXPERIENCE the four steps presented here, don't just read them and forget about them!

More about the basic **P.A.C.E.** process is discussed in my introductory Power Psychology chapter,

Chapter 1 in this book. Check out that chapter first and when you're finished repeat after me:

*You . . . Are . . . Getting . . . Sleepy . . . Very . . . Sleepy . . . VERY . . .*

No, wait. STOP! Save that for later. Right now, just answer this question: So, how is your sleep?

## G.O.O.D.!

**G – GET READY** for a good night's sleep. That means PREPARING yourself by settling yourself down 1–2 hours BEFORE you actually get into bed. Typically, exercise, watching TV, playing video games, chatting online and similar behaviors ACTIVATE your attention, not reduce it.

This is most likely because of the LIGHT that is flooding into your eyes and the psychological ACTIVITY that you are using to concentrate and pay attention. At night, however, the goal is to sleep, not pump yourself up for more activity. People who work the night shift or in restaurants or night clubs know this — coming home after a night of working, you just can't go to sleep right away.

Most people need a "winding down" period before they can get to sleep. We all have a natural rhythm to our sleep and when we disrupt that rhythm, either because of work, illness or bad habits, our natural sleep cycle (commonly referred to as our "circadian rhythm") is disrupted and we just can't get to sleep the way we used to. Our job is to reverse that cycle and get ourselves back on track.

---

*Psych Note! The techniques mentioned in this chapter are generally considered in the category of "sleep hygiene." That just means a WHOLE lot about poor sleeping has to do with our own BEHAVIOR and not some deep-seated medical problem or illness.*

*But poor sleeping can be the result of a medical problem, for example, having a cold or flu. But poor sleep can also be caused by psychological problems such as DEPRESSION, ANXIETY or PANIC Disorders — heck, almost ANY behavior can be caused by a psychological problem!*

*So if you have been having poor sleep for two weeks or longer, it is really a good idea to consult a psychologist or physician for an assessment to be sure that your sleeping problems are not just a symptom of a bigger psychological or medical problem.*

---

O – ONLY SLEEP when you are in bed. Many people read, watch television, talk to friends, eat and otherwise socialize in their bed. That's a no-no when you have a sleeping problem. If you can't sleep, then it is commonly recommended that you get out of bed after about 20–30 minutes of lying awake and sit in a chair to read or think.

But DON'T lie in bed thinking about how you can't sleep or watching the clock move minute by minute.

DO NOT think about how much sleep you are losing, how you need to be rested for work in the morning or worry about bills, life or . . . how you are not getting any good quality sleep!

You have to "retrain" your body that sleep time is for sleeping, not anything else, and the bed is not a library.

**O – O**VERSLEEPING is a no-no. "How can I do that," you might wonder, "when I can't get any sleep at all?" Well, actually, you ARE getting sleep, but you probably aren't thinking about it.

People who don't sleep at night usually sleep . . . during the day! They'll "catch up" by taking naps during the day, usually during monotonous activity like subway or bus rides to and from work, math class, business meetings and so forth. As long as you don't miss your bus stop or get caught napping, a few NAPS ARE OK.

But when you are having sleeping problems, **O**VERSLEEPING (sleeping a little bit here and there when you should be doing AWAKE activities) actually can PREVENT you from sleeping at night.

Nearly every parent knows that letting a young child nap too late in the day results in a cranky little kid who is OVERTIRED because the child's own circadian rhythm has been disrupted and the poor, tired child WANTS to sleep, but now can't when the regular bedtime comes. Sound familiar?

ADULTS get cranky and overtired also when they miss their own normal bedtimes. So try NOT to nap late in the afternoon or early evening when you have a nighttime sleep problem.

If you DON'T have a sleep problem, daytime napping is usually just fine.

**D – DON'T POP PILLS! EVER.** When folks have trouble sleeping, there is a real impulse to just "take something" to get to sleep. The problem is, there are VERY few medications that help provide real, restorative sleep.

The prescription medications you can get are meant to provide some relief for a few nights on a limited basis and do not work for everyone. When a pill doesn't work, however, folks usually think, "Well, maybe one wasn't strong enough; maybe another one will help."

WRONG!

Sleep meds are usually VERY powerful and an overdose can KILL YOU. If the prescribed dosage doesn't help, CALL YOUR DOCTOR and discuss it.

Over-the-counter remedies are often available, but many people find them of little use, so, again, they think, "Hmm, maybe I need to take more." WRONG AGAIN — you can also get ill, sometimes VERY ILL, or DIE from overdosing on some drugstore drugs.

DON'T POP PILLS! EVER!

Sure you need to sleep, but not FOREVER! Wait until morning and consult a professional for help.

---

*Psych Note!* *There are so-called "natural" remedies that some people have found helpful, but, again, not everyone finds them helpful. Consulting an MD (Medical Doctor) is usually where people start when seeking help for insomnia, but a sleep doctor (often a qualified psychologist or MD with specialized training) is a better choice.*

*Many states also license NDs (Naturopathic Doctors) who specialize in natural remedies more than the pharmaceutical drugs that MDs usually prescribe. The point is, consult a specialist, someone who CAN HELP you, rather than going it alone if regular sleep hygiene changes do not help.*

*Sleep problems MAY BE due to SLEEP APNEA (a condition where people can't breathe during the night), SNORING or even a PRIMARY INSOMNIA or other psychological or medical problem. If your sleep doesn't improve with the use of sleep hygiene techniques, consult a professional. Really.*

---

## Your Turn Starts Now!

**PTL** is about taking what science has learned in the laboratories and putting it to use in your own life, in the real world, starting today. You need to take what you learn from **PTL** and PUT IT INTO PRACTICE IN YOUR LIFE.

Don't just THINK about what you've read so far — USE IT, DO IT, PRACTICE IT and do so CONSISTENTLY.

Remember, the more time you spend working on a task — working on it CORRECTLY, that is — the more likely you are to be successful at accomplishing that task. THINKING is very important and is ALWAYS a good place to start any activity, but thinking without ACTION will not change your life very much. It is the EXPERIENCE of putting positive thoughts into positive actions that can improve our quality of life.

**PTL** is a program where you can't lose — you can just win. If you skip or miss a day or make a mistake, just pick up where you left off and keep going forward. If you've stopped or dropped out of a program — just start again. YOU CAN DO THIS! YES, YOU!

All you need to get started is your brain — and, fortunately, you just happen to have it with you right now! How handy is that?

Get that brain working and **GET PREPARED** to sleep; **ONLY** lie in bed for about 20 minutes and then get up if you are not sleepy or close to sleep; do not **OVERSLEEP**, but let your increasing drowsiness during the day help re-set your internal clock for nighttime sleep; and, above all, **DON'T** become someone who habitually POPS PILLS to try and get to sleep. **G.O.O.D.!**

You can START RIGHT NOW (well, OK, in this case, wait until bedtime) and how will you soon be sleeping? **G.O.O.D.**

## *T.A.F.N. . . .*

That's **A**ll **F**or **N**ow — Whew, isn't that enough? Whenever you're ready for more, check out the next chapter in this book that interests you.

Until then, *G.O.O.D. night* . . . .

# *NOTES*

*"The greatest weapon against stress is our ability to choose one thought over another."*
*–William James*

# Chapter 10

## *Using Power Psychology to Help Stop Worrying*

### *What Is "Power Psychology"?*

It is a simple solution to complex personal problems. Psychology is the science of understanding human behavior. Human behavior, of course, is complex and what seems obvious is not always the case. People have been studying — and trying to improve — human behavior since the philosopher Epictetus lectured in the public square of ancient Greece and it is often considered that the European struggle between religion and philosophy was the beginning of modern psychology.

We've come a long way since then and modern science, such as Magnetic Resonance Imaging (MRI), Positron Emission Tomography (PET) and a veritable alphabet soup of other diagnostic assessment tools, has

continued to show that human behavior is caused by "hidden psychological processes." This is just a fancy way of saying, "stuff we do that we usually don't think about very much."

Power Psychology is simply a way of taking what scientists have found out in their laboratories about our "hidden psychological processes" and bringing it OUT of the laboratories and giving it to people in a way they can use in the real world. Why? So people can put "research" to use in their own lives to make real and powerful changes in their own — and others' — behavior to improve the quality of their own lives — and the lives of the people they love. We take these powerful scientific psychological techniques and turn them into **Power Psychology Techniques for Living (PTL)**.

Using **Power Psychology Techniques for Living** can help you change your life for the better. Applying **PTL** to everyday actions and events in your life can improve results in so many areas — health, relationships, income, longevity — the list is probably only limited by your imagination.

This section, Chapter 10 in this book of **Power Psychology Techniques for Living**, focuses upon how to use **PTL** to help you learn to stop worrying.

### *When Can I Get Started?*

Right now. There are always only FOUR STEPS to learning a particular set of **PTL**. Each chapter in the

**PTL** series is written to be a "stand-alone" chapter, which means that you can read each chapter alone and in any order you wish to learn the particular set of **PTL** that applies to the subject. You don't have to read each chapter starting from the first chapter in the series to the last in order to get a benefit from any chapter.

Each chapter builds on the previous chapters, however, and the more chapters you read, the more **PTL** you can learn to apply in your life. This chapter doesn't give you tips on anxiety and panic treatment, because it assumes that you ALREADY HAVE a therapist and are getting treatment IF you know you HAVE anxiety and panic issues. This chapter helps you learn to use **PTL** to worry less and focus on more positive life experiences RIGHT NOW.

## *How Can Power Psychology Help Me Stop Worrying?*

First, as always, remember to **P.A.C.E.** yourself. That means, **PRACTICE** what you learn here; be **AWARE** of the environment in which you practice; **COGITATE** (think) about what you are doing; and actually **EXPERIENCE** the four steps presented here, don't just read them and forget about them!

More about the basic **P.A.C.E.** process is discussed in my introductory Power Psychology chapter, Chapter 1 in this book. Then, when you're ready to face your worries — **H.A.H.A.**!

## *What, You Worry? H.A.H.A.!*

**H** – **HAVE A LAUGH.** I know — how can you laugh when you're so worried? Here's the secret: Research shows that laughing, even for just a few moments, actually turns off that part of our brain system that triggers what people label as an anxiety response.

Well, THAT'S a no-brainer, right? Well, how about this? The same research shows us that even FAKE LAUGHTER, like just forcing a fake belly laugh when there is NOTHING funny going on at all, gives your brain the SAME benefit it gets from a real laugh! HA! Take THAT, worry monster!

When you start to feel worried — just (fake) laugh it off! No, really. You just CAN'T BE worried and NOT WORRIED at the same time. One behavior "turns off" the other: Worry turns off a laugh and a laugh, even a fake one, turns off worry!

---

*Psych Note! This technique has to do with something called the "Sympathetic Nervous System" and the "Para-sympathetic Nervous System," and this chapter is too short to review the exact research findings. But trust me, it's true. And also trust me on this: It feels really weird the first few times you fake a belly laugh! And it works — there are even special yoga programs called "Laugh Yoga." You can do this — heck, the actors on your favorite TV shows do fake laughing all the time! If they can do it, you can, too. So do it!*

---

**A** - ASSESS what you are worried about. Usually, worriers worry about things they have no control over and "no control" is the key here. If you are worried about something that you DO HAVE some control over, then focus on how you can actually solve the problem or issue that you are worried about — that goes a long, long way toward reducing your worries! If you genuinely DO NOT HAVE any control over what is making you worry — then why worry about it at all?

Conrad Hilton, the hotel magnate, wrote in his biography how he dealt with his worry over completing the first really big deal he made in his early days. He essentially said, "I had done everything I could think of to make this deal happen. I checked and rechecked everything. I did everything I could do. But then I was done. Either it was going to happen or not — there was nothing else I could do about it."

Realizing that there was nothing else he could do, what did he do? He went on a small vacation until it was time to see if the deal would actually be completed! He came back in plenty of time before the deal was to go through, of course.

His partners and helpers, unfortunately, kept right on worrying and worried even more when they found out that Mr. Hilton was just going to leave everything and go on vacation! But ol' Conrad was right. He even quoted a passage from the Bible as his reasoning: "Having done all, stand." He took that to mean, "Look, when you've done EVERYTHING that you can possibly do about something, then just stop 'doing' already. To keep 'doing' would only be counter-productive and just be 'busy-work,' not productive or helpful at all. Just stop."

Worrying is not productive and not helpful at all. Just stop.

**H – HAVE A PLAN.** And then work your plan! Recognize when you are starting to worry. Worriers have predictable "triggers" that are "early warning systems" that worry is about to start.

Learn what YOUR "worry-triggers" are and then, when you notice they are starting, stop them before your worries get bigger.

An example of this is the old saying, "Don't make a mountain out of a mole hill." That is, keep things in perspective.

Have a plan: Do what needs to be done when you have control over worrisome matters.

Don't bother worrying when you have no control over matters. If worry-triggers occur, use a relaxation program like the **P.A.C.E.** program mentioned above or some other program (there are literally hundreds available to choose from).

Finally, REMIND yourself that you HAVE A PLAN in place to combat worrying and USE IT!

*Psych Note! Relaxation programs range from simple deep breathing to yoga to "mindfulness" to meditation to self-hypnosis to . . . WOW, the list is VERY long. This short chapter isn't long enough to list them all or to recommend the "best" ones.*

*But I will tell you this: It really doesn't matter WHAT program you use to teach yourself how to relax — use any one you want! The "best" relaxation program is the one that teaches you how to relax yourself and that you will use over and over again. Just find one and use it!*

**A** – GET AWAY FROM WORRIES! No, I don't mean run away from your responsibilities or take many vacations (sorry for the bad news . . .). What I mean is that you should have many things that occupy your mind — lots of hobbies, lots of tasks, lots of interests, and lots of meaningful things going on in your life.

Worriers tend to worry when they have nothing else to set their minds on. That's right — if your mind doesn't have something else to do, chances are — it's gonna FIND something to do and that's like . . . "Hmmm, I'm gonna . . . well, um . . . let's see . . . what is there to . . . OH! I KNOW! I'LL WORRY ABOUT (whatEVER!)."

No kidding; this is how the mind works. If it doesn't have something to focus upon, it'll FIND something to focus on and guess what's an easy and handy thing to occupy an idle mind? Yep, that's right: Worry.

But DON'T YOU worry — this WON'T happen to you . . . anymore. When worries come . . . **H.A.H.A.!**

## *Your Turn Starts Now!*

**PTL** is about taking what science has learned in the laboratories and putting it to use in your own life, in the real world, starting today. You need to take what you learn from **PTL** and PUT IT INTO PRACTICE IN YOUR LIFE. Don't just THINK about what you've read so far — USE IT, DO IT, PRACTICE IT and do so CONSISTENTLY.

Remember, the more time you spend working on a task — working on it CORRECTLY, that is — the more likely you are to be successful at accomplishing that task. THINKING is very important and is ALWAYS a good place to start any activity, but thinking without ACTION will not change your life very much. It is the EXPERIENCE of putting positive thoughts into positive actions that can improve our quality of life.

**PTL** is a program where you can't lose — you can just win. If you skip or miss a day or make a mistake, just pick up where you left off and keep going forward. If you've stopped or dropped out of a program — just start again. YOU CAN DO THIS! YES, YOU!

All you need to get started is your brain — and, fortunately, you just happen to have it with you right now! How handy is that? Get that brain working and **H**AVE A LAUGH; **A**SSESS what's worrying you; **H**AVE A PLAN on how to deal with worry and GET **A**WAY FROM WORRIES by having more interesting things to do besides worry!

## *T.A.F.N.* . . .

That's **A**ll **F**or **N**ow — Whew, isn't that enough? Whenever you're ready for more, check out the next chapter in this book that interests you. If you've read this whole book, cover to cover, *Congratulations!*

Read it again.

# *NOTES*

# Afterword

The hardest part of putting a book together is not what to put in, but what to leave out. If every book contained everything about a subject that the author knew, each book would be about a thousand pages of very small type, and maybe even more.

That dilemma is especially acute when writing about psychology. The field is so broad, even the sub-field of clinical psychology is so comprehensive, that no amount of inclusion can provide the helpful information that everyone might need.

But the solution that I have is simple, if not elegant. My message is that everyone can benefit from visiting a qualified, experienced, well-trained and educated psychologist — if for no other reason than to be assured that no "masked" or "hidden" psychological issues are hard at work undermining an individual's health or welfare or that of their family and loved ones.

But that's never going to happen. Either because the people who most need the help that a psychologist can offer are probably the least likely to *want* to see a psychologist or that there is no such psychologist *available* to the people who earnestly do want help to have a better, happier and healthier life. It's a big world, after all, not a small one and it's one where behavioral and medical health care resources are very unevenly distributed.

So my goal in writing this book is to encourage readers to think about their lives and how it's all going for them and their families.

If it's not going as well as you think it should or could be going, maybe it's time to think that a previously unsuspected verbal or nonverbal learning disability may be at work in your life or maybe you are clinically depressed or are experiencing the lingering effects of trauma.

Perhaps you are experiencing an undiagnosed condition like Attention Deficit Hyperactivity Disorder, Oppositional Defiant Disorder, Tourette's Syndrome or any of a hundred other behavioral, personality or medical problems that could lead to low energy, sleeping problems, relationship difficulties, academic or work failure or repeated involvement with the legal system.

These are not easy issues to consider and some may prefer to avoid such considerations altogether, but the alternative is to remain at the mercy of half-truths, ignorance and helplessness.

But you don't have to do that anymore. The more education, information and knowledge one has, the more help and hope one has.

Nobody and nothing is perfect or lasts forever, but we all can share the aspirational goal of being the best that we can become, if not for ourselves, then for the people we love or for our children and also our grandchildren and our great-grandchildren.

Hope for the future doesn't just mean our *own* future, but *their* future as well.

Best wishes,

Michael Abruzzese, Ph.D.
*Osterville, MA*
*September 7, 2013*

# So, How Did It Go?

I wrote this book to show how applying psychological techniques can help improve people's lives: Has it helped you? I'd love to hear from you — and I think my other readers would, too.

Do you have a story about how this book has helped you that you would like to share?

Do you have a suggestion that could improve future editions of this book?

If so, contact me at DrA@vistahealth.cc.

You can share your story, sign up for my newsletter, and access pre-publication sales of other books in the *TEN LESSONS* series.

Visit **www.TenLessons.org** to learn more.

*Thanks for reading!*

# Order Form

*Just complete this order and get it to us somehow . . .*

**BY FAX:** 815-346-5309

**BY PHONE:** 508-775-6766

**BY E-MAIL:** info@vistahealth.cc

**BY POSTAL SERVICE:** Vista Health Services, Inc., Order Department, PO Box 1060, Osterville, MA 02655, USA.

Please send me *10 Lessons for Using Power Psychology* at $19.95. I understand that I may return it for a full refund for any reason, at any time. How great is that?

Name:_____

Address: _____

City: _____

State: _____ Zip Code: _____

Phone: _____

E-mail: _____

**Sales Tax:** Add 6.25% for orders shipped to Massachusetts.

**Shipping in the U.S.:** Please add $4.00 for the first item ordered and $2.00 for each additional one.

**International:** Add $10.00 for each item ordered.

Our books are typically available in ebook form, large print and paperback from the usual sources, including our own website:
*http://www.TenLessons.org*

*Vista Health Services, Inc.*

*www.TenLessons.org*

*www.TotalSchoolSuccess.com*

*www.DrAplus.com*

# Gift Certificate

## Thanks for buying this book!

As my personal thanks, I am giving you this Gift Certificate entitling you to a 25% discount off your gift purchase of this book for someone you know who may be interested in reading these TEN LESSONS.

Simply send this page (no photocopies, please), a copy of your proof of the purchase of this book and a check for $15.00 (that includes shipping charges) and we'll send a copy of TEN LESSONS to the person you name, with a note saying the book came from you, and add both names to our TEN SERIES mailing list for future notifications. How great is that?

My Name: _____

My Address: _____

_____

My Phone (for confirmation purposes): _____

Please Send a Copy of this Book to My

Friend: _____

At: _____

_____

Send This Form to:

Vista Health Services, Inc.
PO Box 1060
Osterville, MA 02655

*"It's all good."*
*—William Wadoski*

Made in the USA
Middletown, DE
12 August 2015